Not Of This World

A Catholic Guide to Minimalism

STERLING JAQUITH

DEDICATION

This book is dedicated to all the holy men and women who take a vow of poverty, spending their lives in prayer and service to others.

And as always, to the Blessed Mother who watches over all of her children

CONTENTS

Problem Solving Real Life Challenges

The Latin word for "stuff" is "impedimentum" from which we get the word "impediment" so the essential meaning of "stuff" is that it holds us back or gets in the way of living our lives.

HOW TO USE THIS BOOK

This book is meant to take you on a journey. You may immerse yourself in this journey completely until you have overhauled your home and your philosophy, or you may find that you need to take baby steps each weekend as you dip your toes into the world of minimalism. Below are the three major sections of the book. You can read them in order or skip straight to a section you need now.

Not Of This World
Why Catholics Should Embrace Minimalism

This part of the book lays the foundation for WHY we should be doing this at all. If you think minimalism is simply about cleaning and organizing, you're missing the depth and the beauty of choosing this lifestyle. Start with this section of the book. We must anchor our desires in Christ and understand why embracing minimalism is an important aspect of living out our Catholic faith.

The Process
Steps to a Minimalist Lifestyle

This part of the book is the HOW TO section. Here you will find the questions we need to ask ourselves about every room in our home and every item we choose to keep. All the worksheets associated with this process can be printed off at www.sterlingjaquith.com/minimalism.

The Nitty Gritty
Problem Solving Real Life Challenges

This part of the book answers the WHAT IF questions you have. What if you have nine children? What if you are barely able to afford your grocery budget? What if you have a blended family where step-children only live in the house every other weekend? What if you need to save years' worth of homeschooling curriculum? You can flip to a specific topic or read through them all!

Sterling Jaquith

Not Of This World: Why Catholics Should Embrace Minimalism

CHAPTER 1:
WHAT IS MINIMALISM?

Some of you may be very familiar with the philosophy of minimalism and perhaps have practiced it for many years. Some of you may have no idea what it is, and this book landed in your lap unexpectedly. Let me take a quick moment to explain the idea of minimalism and then we'll dive into why I believe all Catholics should embrace this way of living.

You may have the idea that minimalism is about living in a studio apartment, giving up most of your stuff, and having only gray, modern furniture. For most of us, that isn't attractive and certainly doesn't seem to be compatible with having a large or homeschooled family! Thankfully, this isn't what minimalism is about at all. There aren't rigid rules about how to live a minimalist lifestyle. It's not about the number of things you own or the way you organize your stuff.

Instead, it is a philosophy, a state of mind. It's about living intentionally. Minimalism is about choosing where we put our focus, our money, and our time.

One of my favorite definitions of minimalism comes from Joshua Becker who has written many books on the subject.

"...minimalism is the intentional promotion of the things we most value and the removal of everything that distracts us from it. It is a life that forces intentionality. And as a result, it forces improvements in almost all aspects of your life."

I find this to be very much like the journey of our Catholic faith, both in trying to discern the will of God for our lives and with our mission to become saints! As I seek to live out my Catholic faith and to strive for sainthood, I don't want to surround myself with things, people, or appointments that get in the way of that mission.

I want to serve the Lord and lead others to Him. I want to live a life of service to my family, my community, and especially the poor. I believe the best way we can do that is by living intentionally.

Here are some ways that many of us are not living intentionally:

- We have filled our calendars with too many appointments at the sacrifice of our faith and time with our family.
- We have 43 pairs of shoes but we really only wear 7 of them often.
- There are at least 3 "stacks" of papers in your home, many including important bills or documents that need to be dealt with.
- We check our phone more than 50 times per day for updates.
- There are bins of craft items living in our closet that we will definitely use "one day."
- We can't park our cars in the garage because it is full.
- We constantly feel like we need more money and a bigger house just to manage our lives.
- We are living in a constant state of worry and anxiety.

Lori Lippincott, the author of Simple Living, says, "Being a minimalist isn't a ticket into an elite group or defined by a specific number of possessions. Being a minimalist is something that starts in the mind and is driven by intangibles. The visible and tangible is only a byproduct of **intentional living decisions.**"

She goes on to say, "Minimalists are priority centered. [They] know or are trying to find out what is most important to them and live their life based on that information."

Minimalism is not just about cleaning and decluttering our homes. It's about honestly asking ourselves, "Do I need all this stuff? Am I planning my week intentionally or am I just reacting to what shows up? Am I trying to keep up with the Jones's and is it stealing my peace? Do I spend more time focused on decorating and shopping than I do growing in my faith? Am I wasting a lot of time searching through piles to find the things I need?"

We must be intentional about the things we own, what we think about, and what we choose to do with our time. We must be good stewards of what God has given us including our bodies, the people He puts in our path, and the things He has allowed us to acquire. We must view everything as a tool for the glory of God.

Though there are many practical benefits of a minimalist lifestyle, there are a lot of spiritual benefits as well. Imagine a life where everything you owned had a place, and you were perfectly content with what was in your home. Because you had less stuff to take care of and clean, you could spend more time with your family and more time pursuing your passions and deepening your faith.

What if you used your money to purchase fewer but higher-quality things for your family instead of acquiring dozens of cheap plastic items that eventually get thrown away?

Imagine a life where you had more peace.

Imagine a life where you had more freedom.

That is my hope for you.

I believe this is possible for all of us whether we have large families, live in studio apartments, homeschool our children, are living on a tight budget, are single, or are living in a state of transition right now.

CHAPTER 2:
IN THE WORLD

Because I grew up with a single mother and little money, I am very familiar with the feeling of being left out, of not being cool enough, and of the pain that comes when you realize your home, your shoes, your music collection, your phone is…less than. I'm not sure when we become aware of this arbitrary measuring process that happens among peers, but from a young age, we begin to master the skill of comparing and then compensating.

I got my first job when I was 14 and immediately began to use my money to hide my family origins and our financial instability. If I too can afford clothes from the Gap and the latest CD's (these were cool in the 90's) then maybe *they* will want to be my friend. I don't even remember who "they" are and that's the sad result of hoping conformity and materialism will form genuine relationships. It never lasts.

I'd like to say that when I encountered Jesus and became Catholic, I suddenly saw the error of my J.Crew loving ways and living life paycheck to paycheck… that I threw myself into His arms and said, "You are enough for me Lord!" But that's not what happened at all.

I simply looked around at the other Catholics to quickly figure out what their lingo was and what clothes, books, and hobbies would help me fit in with this new group. Almost immediately, after getting pregnant, this evolves into wading through parenting philosophies, baby gadgets, and constantly asking if I'm doing the "right things" or if I have the "right things" to raise my children well.

This is exhausting, it's never-ending, and it's deeply unsatisfying.

Fr. John Burns captures this sentiment well when he says, "Too easily, we let ourselves obsess about an unattainable horizon of perfection, an idea we create by cobbling together all the "greatest hits" of things we see in others. As we do, we implicitly tell God (and ourselves) that what we have is simply not enough."[i]

And here we encounter the truth. Rarely is our pursuit of stuff, hobbies, or achievements about God. We are caught up in a swirl of self-centered doubt, "Am I good enough? Do they really like me? Am I missing out on something better?" We allow the noise of our own thoughts and the noise of the world around us to drown out the loving whispers of the Lord. We are easily pulled from His grasp. The further we are from Him, the more emptiness we feel inside.

Most of us feel a deep sense of being unfulfilled. We feel as if we're getting something wrong, that we're missing out on something more. Mistakenly we double down on chasing things of this world, often noble-sounding things like activities for our children, a nice home for our family, volunteering for church, etc. While there can be goodness found in all of those things, likely we are pursuing them for the wrong reasons.

We are desperate to create enough distractions to avoid the pain we feel inside, and we stuff in as many pleasures as we can hoping they will feed the gnawing hunger we have.

But we are not of this world.

Nothing in this world will ever fully satisfy us. Our ultimate desire will always be for God, and that is why I believe all Catholics should embrace a lifestyle of minimalism. This doesn't mean getting rid of everything we own and spending 8 hours of our day praying. It means turning our mind and our heart to God and constantly asking Him, "Does this bring You glory?"

Let us live intentionally for our Creator. Let us search for peace in His arms. We've done it the other way and it's left us exhausted, confused, and depressed. We need to break the chains that the world has around us and learn how to be in the world but not of it. This book will show you exactly how to do that no matter what life stage you're in or what lifestyle you have.

CHAPTER 3:
FREEDOM

After my grandmother passed and my family came face-to-face with the reality left behind by a hoarder, I began to be interested in the idea of minimalism. I read a few articles about minimalism but it seemed like such a huge lifestyle change that I didn't know where to begin. I'd bookmark a few ideas then soon forget about them.

Then I would find myself running frantically through the house looking for something. Where is it? Why can't I find it? I'm going to be so late! Other days I would feel overwhelmed by the task of being a homemaker. How do I keep this house clean? I need a good system. If I just had the right organizing tools, things would be better.

More and more, I catch myself thinking, "If we had less

stuff, life would be easier."

Intuitively, I understood that owning fewer things would require less work and would bring me more peace. I didn't realize, however, that simply thinking less often about my stuff would also bring me peace. I decided I wanted to learn more about minimalism to see if it could help me feel less frazzled.

The more I read about a minimalist lifestyle, the more I was drawn to it. It sounded a lot like the challenge in my first book, *Catholic Mom Challenge* – live intentionally, figure out systems that work, get rid of things you don't need, and focus on what's important in your life. And yet, as much of this resonated with me, it surprised me that few people were making the connection of decluttering and detaching our lives with connecting to Jesus.

It became clear to me that God, who designed each of us to be like Him and to love one another, would discourage us from getting too comfortable and valuing things above people. We are to be in this world, not of it.

But just as I saw a lack of Christianity in the minimalist message, I also saw three very big lifestyles that were rarely addressed: large families, homeschooling families, and the poor. How were these groups of people to practice minimalism?

I decided to write a book that puts Jesus at the center of our desire to live a minimalistic lifestyle and also address the specific needs of these lifestyles. My hope is that by providing practical solutions, Catholic families can find a way to detach themselves from their stuff and anchor their lives with Christ instead.

As we love Him more, we store up more treasure in Heaven, which is the best kind of treasure and truly, the only kind that lasts.

This will not be an easy journey for most of us. My hope is

that this book will act as an accountability partner, a friend to hold your hand along the way as we challenge our own ideas about the stuff we own and the way we spend our time.

No one wants to admit that they are owned by their possessions. We want to think we're in control of our "stuff situation." I was shocked when I read these statements from the Simple and Soul blog just how owned I was by my things:

If you turn down invitations because you need to be home cleaning or organizing…**you're owned.**

If you are unable to pursue your passion because your debt has you working overtime every month…**you're owned.**

If you feel overwhelmed and ashamed by the clutter in your home or office…**you're owned.**

If you feel secure and satisfied after a purchase and within days feel the letdown of disappointment… **you're owned.**

Is this the life we want to live for the next few decades we may have left in this life?[ii]

If you're starting to feel uncomfortable, that's good. It's honest, and it's real. We cannot make a permanent change if we're lying to ourselves about our unhealthy attachment to the things we own. I want to be free to love Jesus more than anything else in the world. I want to be free to become the person He desires me to be. I want to be free to cherish the people I love.

This freedom does not come easily, we have to work hard — sometimes against ourselves. For many of us who hoard our things or overbook our calendar, it's likely that, deep down, fear is our true motivator.

- We fear we'll never be able to afford a new pair of shoes.
- We fear that we'll miss out or our children will miss out by not attending all the activities we're invited to.
- We fear that we will get pregnant again and need the host of items that ease the transition of a newborn into the family.
- We fear that our only connection to loved ones who have died are found in sentimental items we keep to remember them.
- We fear that if we don't have the right things, we won't be accepted, we won't have friends, or we won't be loved.

Whatever it is that we fear we will lose is nothing compared to our salvation and living for eternity in Heaven. Jesus did not come into the world so that we could live a life of fear. He came that we should live an abundant life!

As we peel back our worries and concerns, we often discover our own lack of trust in God. Sometimes we have to look under our piles of stuff to realize that we've been clinging to our possessions instead of our faith. We can find freedom by letting go of our things.

CHAPTER 4:
A STORY OF TWO HOARDERS

Our body has this defect that, the more it is provided care and comforts, the more needs and desires it finds. -St. Teresa of Avila

Before getting married, my husband and I talked about finances, budgeting, and the kind of parents we wanted to be. We did not, however, talk about our philosophy on stuff. It didn't occur to us to talk about how we were going to take care of the things that we own. Like many habits in marriage, we were blissfully unaware we might take different approaches to storing our things.

Later in this book, I will discuss how to work with your spouse when the two of you are not on the same page about stuff management. Thankfully, both my husband and I had experiences with grandparents who were hoarders and this greatly shaped our views of what we would keep in our home. We agreed that less is more.

Despite being on the same page with this simple mantra, it was actually much harder to maintain a "less is more" lifestyle than we thought. This became even truer when we started making more money and having kids. I'll talk later about the systems we've put in place and also what we did when we suddenly found ourselves with very little money to live on.

To understand our great commitment to minimalism, I'd like to share two stories from our family. Though my husband and I witnessed two very different kinds of hoarding, each of these homes that took hours upon hours to clear out showed us how consumerism, misplaced sentimentality, and fear can spiral out of control.

Juanita

My grandmother grew up extremely poor. Her parents dropped her off at a farm with a family who had agreed to take care of her. But instead of welcoming her into the family with the other children, my grandmother was made to live in their barn. She was given very little food and suffered from rickets because of malnutrition. I can't even begin to imagine what her childhood was like lacking in warmth, love, safety, and comfort.

I have a huge respect for my grandmother because she clawed her way out of poverty by working hard and educating herself. She put herself through college hand-sewing evening gowns for sorority sisters and teaching swimming lessons in the summer. She earned a master's degree in education and would go on to be a special education teacher for more than 50 years. While many in the school district saw how selflessly she gave to her students, few of them knew that she would go home alone filling the hole inside of her with stuff from Costco, Target, the mall, and baubles from the Home Shopping Network.

It's important to understand that living a life without Christ always leaves a hole inside of us.

When she passed away in 2015, she owned a beautiful 2,500 square foot house on a golf course and a shiny (nearly new) fully loaded Acura MDX. Both of which were almost completely financed.

Nearly every single closet, the garage, the attic, and most of the upstairs bedrooms were completely packed with stuff. Unlike some of the hoarders you see on television, my grandmother's house was extremely clean. The majority of what

Sterling Jaquith

she hoarded was kept in pristine boxes with receipts or tags attached.

The downstairs of her home was tidy and welcoming. Other than one or two display cases in each room featuring wooden horses or Faberge eggs, guests would not have any idea the amount of stuff that was bulging from behind closed doors or cabinets.

When she passed and we began to tackle the task of clearing out her home, I was overcome with sadness. As I walked through her house, which felt like a department store, I imagined that scared little girl who slept so many nights on the floor of a barn always lived inside of her. I imagined she told herself, "Never again will I be poor and helpless." My grandmother was a very strong woman, but she also had a great brokenness inside of her.

She did not have a relationship with Jesus. I have no doubt she was exposed to a broken and perhaps even abusive version of Catholicism in her youth. As an adult, I never knew her to go to church, and though we can never know what's in someone's heart, I doubt she had any form of a prayer life.

She believed the lie that stuff would make her happy; that accumulating wealth (even in the form of collectible plates) would fill the hole inside of her.

She genuinely thought that she was buying things that were collectible and that would become more valuable in the future. She had thousands of dolls including three-foot-tall porcelain dolls and hundreds of Barbies. She had a few hundred Beanie Babies. She owned a beautiful Faberge egg collection and at least a hundred hand-painted wooden horses. She was convinced these things would be worth a fortune.

In the end, almost everything she owned was sold at an estate sale for next to nothing. It took weeks to organize everything and many weekends donating what didn't sell. The treasure she stored up would not help her children as she intended but instead would be a huge burden and provide a glimpse into how empty her life must have really been to feel the need to keep buying such useless things.

Her kitchen was packed with food, and her closet was packed with clothes, many from Nordstrom that still had tags on them. As my family stared at the work ahead of us, instead of feeling angry, I felt sad. I was sad for that little girl inside of my grandmother who must have been so scared and lonely.

My grandmother spent countless hours and hundreds of thousands of dollars trying to soothe her fear by trying to buy comfort and security.

Don't be confused, this level of hoarding is not just a hobby gone wrong, it's a sickness. It's a disease, and like many addictions, it's extremely difficult to just stop. Most of us do not suffer from this kind of clinical hoarding, but it is easy for us to get together and collectively acknowledge, "Whoa that's a problem. No one should accumulate that much stuff." This truth is important for us to remember as we evaluate our own homes and find echoes of this same brokenness and this same fear in our lives.

We are not of this world, and nothing we own will ever satisfy the restlessness in our hearts.

Ruhl and Norma

My husband also had a set of grandparents who were hoarders. They were both children of poor German immigrants. The importance of saving for the future was firmly taught to both of them. They were married shortly before the great depression and had many very difficult years. Both worked hard, taking any job they could find, and were able to raise their children through the difficult years. Ruhl worked long hours loading cement onto boats at a pier in cold northern Michigan. It was very hard work, and they both suffered through those years – emotionally and nutritionally. Both had many serious health conditions because of severe deprivations during these years.

When the depression ended and life began to get better, they were able to buy more things. They never forgot how difficult life was, so they made sure to save up the basic essentials of life. They would buy dried food to store in the basement until the entire basement was full of packaging. They purchased many freezers to put in the garage so they could store frozen food. They knew the importance of vitamins and bought so many bottles that several bedrooms were packed full of boxes of vitamins.

As they gained more wealth, they realized they could save some of that wealth for the future. Ruhl decided to invest in rare coins and started collecting. Naturally, he realized he could store these coins efficiently in old empty vitamin bottles. Room after room started filling up. As the children left, Norma wanted something to hold on to. Many of the favorite toys were saved. Some were even repurchased so they could be saved. Nothing was sorted, many rooms had mountains of bottles, toys, and papers.

As they aged, the sickness worsened. Now, not only the basics of life but nearly everything was worth saving. They shared this emotional need to be safe, to make sure that neither they nor their children would go through what they went through. Toilet paper, paper towels, paper, pens, all the little things that they couldn't afford during the depression also became important. Finally, as their health worsened, they no longer had the energy to even clean up after themselves. Paper trash was also being added to the piles. Most rooms upstairs were inaccessible. The grandchildren didn't even know that there was a basement, and the garage was also totally off limits.

Norma passed first, and Ruhl lost all drive and passion for life. He slowly wasted away, and his children had to set a schedule to come over to help him stay alive. Despite his lack of care for himself, even still, he could not let go of the things. "You might need them yet; it's best to keep them!" No one was allowed to go upstairs if he was awake. At this point, my husband was in high school. None of the grandchildren wanted to go to that house, but Ruhl's children would drag them over according to schedule.

When Ruhl also passed, the work of cleanup began. Everyone knew it would be bad, but no one expected what they actually found. The garage had nearly a dozen standing freezers packed full of food. Many had not been opened in decades and were frozen into a solid block of ice. After the doors were opened by crowbar, only little corners of mysterious zip-lock bags could be seen sticking out of a solid block of ice. The basement was a vault of molding nastiness. The stairway going upstairs could only be navigated by skinny, nimble people, and the rooms were full from floor to ceiling in one gigantic pile. Even the downstairs rooms had slowly filled up as well. It was like excavating into a mine of garbage.

Cleanup took months. The family rented several large dump bins, but progress was slow. The most frustrating part was the contents were 98% absolute trash, with 2% of rare coins mixed in. Every jar of vitamins or sealed envelope had to be opened to see if it contained rare coins. Eventually, the family gave up, and an outside firm was hired to sort everything. The firm quickly discovered that it cost more to find the coins than the coins were worth. In the end, the entire pile was simply hauled off to a landfill with several big dump trucks. After extensive cleaning, the house was sold for barely more than the estate had spent to empty and clean it.

Ruhl and Norma started with good intentions – wanting to avoid what happened to them before. They wanted to make sure that neither they nor their children would ever suffer such severe deprivation. This fear grew and grew into such a sickness that they simply could not let go of any physical thing, they had to hold on to everything. This fear also passed on to their children. Though not as severe or widespread, each of their children started with attachment. Each has had their own struggle to overcome the same fear of one day going without.

From the outside, this story sounds ridiculous – a pile this big could only be left by crazy people. But I want to challenge all of us – what are we holding on to simply because we are afraid we might desperately need it in the future? We can never find safety in things of this world.

CHAPTER 5:
JESUS WAS THE ULTIMATE MINIMALIST

Without using the term, Christendom has embraced the concept of minimalism consistently since Jesus walked the earth. After all, God sent His only Son to Earth, the King of Kings, and instead of being born in a palace, He was born in a stable. Jesus lived a simple life, first as the son of a carpenter, and then later as a humble traveler bringing His father's truth wherever He went. He did not travel with scores of servants and plush amenities. He relied on the hospitality of others and prayer to sustain Him.

Way before it was trendy, the Disciples and the Apostles chose to live a life of poverty with joy. They relied on the Holy Spirit to guide them and the generosity of the world to house and feed them. Sometimes they were met with warmth and hospitality. Sometimes they were met with martyrdom.

As difficult as this may sound, when you have met the living Son of God and He asks it, I imagine you embrace this vocation joyfully! When you have walked with the son of God, how silly it must seem to quibble about the fashion of your clothes or the number of jewels you own.

This theme of detachment from worldly things appears so many times in the Bible and is so often linked with a deeper spiritual life, that many of the religious orders around the world also take a vow of poverty. Here is a picture of a Carmelite nun reading in her sparsely decorated cell.

A Discalced Carmelite nun by Melchior2006 Wikipedia[iii]

When I look at this picture, I do not feel sorry for her. I do not wish she could be on HGTV and find the perfect decorator to add splashes of color and accent pieces to her room. I see her peace, and I admire it. Deep down I know that I lack this level of peace as I'm surrounded by stuff and noise.

Even those of us whom God does not call to take a vow of poverty can still learn a lot from this example. We don't have to swing so far in the other direction that we allow consumerism and materialism to keep us prisoners; our attentions blocked from the Lord.

The Bible Tells Us So

If you have any doubt that Jesus did not want us to chase after wealth and material possessions, perhaps it is time you dust off your Bible and do some reading. While I don't want to sound like a stodgy minister in the 18th-century railing about money from the pulpit, I think we too often read some of these verses and roll our eyes as if they are old fashioned.

Many of us have convinced ourselves we are not wealthy; we are not the ones chasing money. We claim that we simply want to pay our bills and take care of our family. Yet the success of Starbucks selling $6 coffee and the staggering amount of American credit card debt are both indicators that this isn't true. Most of us are living lives we cannot afford.

Perhaps the wealth we choose includes things like:

- Spending too much money at Target

- Impulse buying at Costco

- Purchasing a house we really couldn't afford

- Financing a new car because we convinced ourselves we could not afford a used one

- Spending hundreds of dollars on subscription boxes

Many of these problems do not plague the wealthy but instead the average, middle-class American family. While we all have different financial situations, we must be honest with ourselves and seek out the ways in which we're clinging to the world instead of clinging to Jesus.

You may feel uncomfortable reading the verses below. Take a deep breath and read them anyway. Let us read them with fresh eyes and challenge our own love of money.

Bible Verses About Wealth and Material Things

For where your treasure is, there your heart will be also.
Matthew 6:21

Whoever loves money never has enough; whoever loves wealth
is never satisfied with their income. This too is meaningless.
Ecclesiastes 5:10

Let no debt remain outstanding, except the continuing debt to
love one another, for whoever loves others has fulfilled the law.
Romans 13:8

Better the little that the righteous have than the wealth of many
wicked; for the power of the wicked will be broken, but the
Lord upholds the righteous. Psalm 37: 16-17

No one can serve two masters. Either you will hate one and
love the other, or you will be devoted to the one and despise the
other. You cannot serve both God and money. Matthew 6:24

For the love of money is a root of all kinds of evil. Some
people, eager for money, have wandered from the faith and
pierced themselves with many griefs. 1 Timothy 6:10

Command those who are rich in this present world not to be
arrogant nor to put their hope in wealth, which is so uncertain,
but to put their hope in God, who richly provides us with
everything for our enjoyment. Command them to do good, to
be rich in good deeds, and to be generous and willing to share.
In this way they will lay up treasure for themselves as a firm
foundation for the coming age, so that they may take hold of
the life that is truly life. 1 Timothy 6: 17-19

If anyone is poor among your fellow Israelites in any of the
towns of the land of the Lord your God is giving you, do not be
hardhearted or tightfisted toward them. Deuteronomy 15:7

Peter answered; "May your money perish with you, because you thought you could buy the gift of God with money!"
Acts 8:20

Jesus sat down opposite the place where the offerings were put and watched the crowd putting their money into the temple treasury. Many rich people threw in large amounts. But a poor widow came and put in two very small copper coins, worth only a few cents. Calling his disciples to him, Jesus said, "Truly I tell you, this poor widow has put more into the treasury than all the others. They all gave out of their wealth; but she, out of her poverty, put in everything—all she had to live on."
Mark 12:41-44

Lazy hands make for poverty, but diligent hands bring wealth.
Proverbs 10:4

You say, "I am rich; I have acquired wealth and do not need a thing.' But you do not realize that you are wretched, pitiful, poor, blind and naked. Revelation 3:17

Suppose one of you wants to build a tower. Won't you first sit down and estimate the cost to see if you have enough money to complete it? Luke 14: 28

"The seed falling among the thorns refers to someone who hears the word, but the worries of this life and the deceitfulness of wealth choke the word, making it unfruitful. Matthew 13:22

The Lord sends poverty and wealth; he humbles and he exalts.
1 Samuel 2:7

Honor the Lord with your wealth, with the firstfruits of all your crops. Proverbs 3:9

CHAPTER 6:
CREATE SPACE

As I began to write this book and share some of my research with my friends, no one questioned why I was working on this project. I was most often met with a deep sigh as a friend would go on to tell me how she too has struggled to get the stuff in her house under control. We intuitively know that we own too many things and that it's holding us back from something better… a life of more contentment.

Ironically, the more unrest we feel, the more we tend to buy to fill the hole; the problem is getting worse and worse each year in America.

"In America, we consume twice as many material goods as we did fifty years ago. Over the same period, the size of the average American home has nearly tripled, and today that average home contains about three hundred thousand items. On average, our homes contain more televisions than people. And the US Department of Energy reports that, due to clutter, 25 percent of people with two-car garages don't have room to park cars inside and another 32 percent have room for only one vehicle. One out of every ten American households rents off-site storage. The average household's credit-card debt stands at over $15,000, while the average mortgage debt is over $150,000."
- The More Of Less by Joshua Becker

Instead of thinking about minimalism as getting rid of a bunch of stuff, think of it as creating more space. Not only are you going to create more space in your home to simply enjoy your family, you're also going to create more space on your calendar for the activities that truly matter, more space in your mind to ponder the things that truly matter, and ultimately more space in your heart for a deep relationship with the Lord.

When was the last time you ran through your house frantically searching for your keys, a piece of mail, a permission slip or something you borrowed from a friend? Maybe it was even this morning. We can clearly picture feeling rushed, frustrated, flipping through piles, shaking out purses, and maybe even yelling through the house asking for help!

This is not simply a problem for people who live in big houses; it's a problem for people who live in clutter and disorganization. We WANT to be better, but we never seem to find the time.

Now imagine you have a place for everything in your home. You know exactly where all your mail is. You have a place for things you need to return to friends. You hang your keys or your purse on a hook every time you come home. I can't promise you will never run around feeling rushed, especially if you have young children who play house and relocate your things inside a plastic teapot in a play kitchen...but I can promise you more peace.

You will have more peace by being in control of your home, your things, and your feelings about everything you own.

Embracing a simpler life isn't just about pleasing Jesus. I honestly believe this philosophy will significantly improve our lives. Having and taking care of less stuff means we'll have more time for our family and more time to pray. Most of us want more peace and contentment in our lives.

We're not just going to create more space to buy better things or get more done throughout the week. We're going to create more space in our lives to connect with the Lord. The better we are at tuning into God, the more we are able to discern His will for our lives. The more we follow His will, the more peace we have and deep down, this is what we all desire.

CHAPTER 7:
EFFICIENCY AND COMFORT

"Paying rapt attention, whether to a trout stream or a novel, a do-it-yourself project or a prayer, increases your capacity for concentration, expands your inner boundaries, and lifts your spirits, but more important, it simply makes you feel that life is worth living." Winifred Gallager, Rapt

Some of you are feeling excited to dive into your home and start decluttering. Some of you are dreading the emotional decisions you're going to have to make. I hope all of you are looking forward to living a simpler, more Christ-focused lifestyle that cultivates peace in your home. As we gear up to embrace a minimalist lifestyle, I want us to watch out for two traps.

Idol of Efficiency

One warning I want to issue, especially to you A-type personalities out there, is the danger of chasing efficiency. Sometimes our desire to not waste time turns into an obsession. We begin to idolize systems and efficiency forsaking people's feelings along the way. We spend so much time trying to save time that we miss out on living our lives with those whom we love.

A few years ago, I decided to take my girls berry picking. It sounded like such a romantic idea... the summer breeze, the sweet berries, and lovely childhood memories! In the end, it was hot, there were lots of bees and spiders, my newly potty-trained toddler pooped in her pants, and the berries ended up costing $25! I drove home thinking, "Ugh, we could have just bought berries at the store for $12 and saved ourselves the trouble!"

My grumpiness, however, showed just how much I had missed the point. I was focused on saving money and saving time. I wanted to avoid the hassle. If you ask my girls, they will say that they love berry picking! They will remember the sweet parts of that day. They chose the better part of being present.

God desires us to be fully present. It's hard to be present when you're worried about "taking the fastest route" or constantly multitasking, trying to slay your to-do list.

If you are looking for ways to be more efficient, let it be so you can have more uninterrupted quality time with your family, not so you can take on more work.

I mean it!

Your goal should be to become efficient about the work you need to do so you can block out more PRAYER TIME, FREE TIME, and QUALITY TIME on your calendar to spend with

Jesus and with your family. Did I get your attention with all the caps?

I have free time, quality time, and prayer time on my schedule. All of those things could look like sitting on the couch from the outside but I know that connecting with the Lord through prayer, drinking a cup of tea by myself, or reading books to my children are all valuable activities.

Our time on earth is limited. We never know when Jesus will call us to our true home. Yes, we must eat, clean our homes, and care for our children but we do not need to live frazzled lives. We do not need to feel stressed searching for solutions to get more done. The solution for our schedules is the same as the solution for our stuff… less is more.

Idol of Comfort

The other big trap we fall into, especially as Americans, is that we idolize comfort. We are always looking for more tools to make us comfortable. If only we had a bigger house, if only we had air conditioning, a nicer mattress, 20 pairs of shoes to guarantee the perfect one for each occasion, a better car with more bells and whistles, this kitchen gadget to save time, etc., life would be better.

Recently it was spring time and we had one hot day among a string of mild ones. The high was 86 degrees, and my husband was out of town with our kids. I was all alone, boiling hot because we hadn't yet switched the house heating/cooling system over to kick on the air conditioning when it was hot outside. As I lay there grumbling for at least a good ten minutes before it finally hit me! My, how quickly I have become entitled to perfect temperatures in my home!

I didn't grow up with air conditioning. I wasn't going to die. It wasn't 105 degrees outside. I had a ceiling fan and the ability to put ice in my water to stay cool. Yes, I was six months pregnant, but really, I wasn't that uncomfortable... I was just slightly uncomfortable.

It can be very easy to chase comfort and suddenly end up with a house full of stuff! We are especially guilty of doing this in the name of children.

- We need five different baby stations to keep the baby happy.
- The kids would play outside more if they had more toys.
- It would be easier for me to take care of the kids if they had an iPad, Netflix, or a LeapFrog tablet.

We hold on to a lot of this stuff because we know that one day, some day, our lives will be made better by the use of this handy-dandy thing.

In the meantime, we live in clutter, and we work long hours to afford the stuff that brings us comfort as well as the house to keep it all.

One lesson I encounter over and over again as I read about the lives of the saints is the idea of embracing suffering. Choosing the harder path as a way to offer up the lack of comfort to Christ. Pope Francis explains suffering to us, "Suffering is a call to conversion: it reminds us of our frailty and vulnerability."

Pope Francis goes on to give us a solution. In 2014, he recommended ten New Year's resolutions including, "Choose the more humble purchase." He adds, "Certainly, possessions, money, and power can give a momentary thrill, the illusion of being happy, but they end up possessing us and making us always want to have more, never satisfied. 'Put on Christ' in your life, place your trust in him, and you will never be disappointed!"[iv]

CHAPTER 8:
THE PSYCHOLOGY OF HOARDING

I want to take a moment and address the psychological disorder of hoarding for two reasons. First, much like a person can have depressing moments without suffering from clinical depression, we can also act like hoarders without suffering from this crippling condition. It's important that we see the signs, the red flags, and the patterns that show us we might be headed for a more serious problem if we do not address our attachment to things before it spirals out of control.

Second, if you suspect that you have a serious problem with hoarding, or that someone you love is a clinical hoarder, you must seek out professional help. It's likely not a problem you can pray your way out of or read enough books to fix. There are likely underlying psychological issues that need to be addressed before you can be free to tackle the piles.

Hoarding both relieves anxiety and produces it. The more hoarders accumulate, the more insulated they feel from the world and its dangers. Of course, the more they accumulate, the more isolated they become from the world, including family and friends. Even the thought of discarding or cleaning out hoarded items produces extreme feelings of panic and discomfort.[v]

Hoarders often feel as if their possessions are actually a part of them. They could no sooner part with their coin collection as if it were one of their very own fingers. We often think of hoarders as messy people, especially if you're seen episodes of A&E's show *Hoarders,* where people often need hazmat suits just to enter a hoarder's home. But, like the case with my grandmother, her house was very neat, orderly, and clean and yet she would become extremely anxious if you even suggested she might not need six different vacuums. She genuinely felt that she did.

The Anxiety and Depression Association of America[vi] lists the following symptoms and behaviors that hoarders might exhibit:

- Inability to throw away possessions
- Severe anxiety when attempting to discard items
- Great difficulty categorizing or organizing possessions
- Indecision about what to keep or where to put things
- Distress, such as feeling overwhelmed or embarrassed by possessions
- Suspicion of other people touching items
- Obsessive thoughts and actions: fear of running out of an item or of needing it in the future; checking the trash for accidentally discarded objects
- Functional impairments, including loss of living space, social isolation, family or marital discord, financial difficulties, health hazards

Some people hold on to items out of fear, perhaps stemming from a time of great poverty in their lives, as Ruhl and Normal did. We see this often with people who lived through the Great Depression. Some people hold onto things because of sentimental value or believing an item is one-of-a-kind and can never be replaced. Some hoarders are simply bargain shoppers. When they see a great sale on hairspray, they buy nine bottles that will then sit in their bathroom for 12 years.

If someone you know does this consistently, seek out a counselor, a therapist, or a priest to help you understand the underlying cause.

CHAPTER 9:
YOUR DOMESTIC CHURCH

"Every home is called to become a 'domestic church' in which family life is completely centered on the lordship of Christ and the love of husband and wife mirrors the mystery of Christ's love for the Church, his bride," Pope Benedict XVI[vii]

If you're reading this book, it's likely that you are in charge of turning your home into a domestic church. As Catholics, we are called to live out our faith, and this must begin in the home.

Whether you have a traditional family, are a single parent, are single, or are discerning religious life, we are all called to make Christ the center of our homes. When someone walks into your home, it should be obvious that you are Catholic and that you love Jesus. This doesn't necessarily mean artwork of saints and Mary all over the house.

Here are some ideas for turning your house into a domestic church:

- Displaying tasteful religious artwork and statues
- Having a home altar
- Keeping prayer books around
- Praying before meals
- Treating all guests with grace and kindness
- Playing soft music sung by nuns or monks in the background
- Having lit candles
- Putting Holy water by the front door

I love this quote from the Boots and Hooves Homestead blog, "When our homes are cluttered, they become distracting and our main goal here is to create a calm environment; one of peace, one which helps us to focus and recollect on our main purpose in this life – that of serving God."[viii] Again, I see so clearly that minimalism and our Catholic faith go hand in hand helping us look to God and to grow in our faith.

I want to teach my children how to live out their faith at home. I want to show them a real example of how to do this day in and day out. My top life goals include getting myself, my husband, and my children to Heaven. I want to give them a little taste of Heaven within the walls of our home. By providing a safe place that points them to the Lord, I know I can arm them for the battle they will face once they go out into the world.

Think of your home as a domestic church; it will help you to better sift through what you own and to keep only which brings glory to God.

CHAPTER 10:
MINIMALISM, DECLUTTERING, AND ORGANIZING

Before diving into the process (and yes, we're almost there!), I want to address the differences between minimalism, decluttering, organizing and cleaning. I'm going to use these four terms a lot throughout the book, and it's important to understand their different meanings.

Minimalism

This is a philosophy. It is a state of mind. It is a lifestyle. Minimalism is the idea that we will choose what we own and what we spend our time on intentionally. We will consider our choices and say, "I believe this brings me value and draws me closer to God." This is a lifelong journey. It's a constant state of being. To embrace minimalism is to continually choose less.

You'll quickly discover that decluttering is not the same thing as minimalism. Hordes of commercial-based websites will tell you how to declutter your closet or your garage but they won't address the psychological reasons we have so much stuff to begin with. We must find our value in God and not in the things we own. By choosing to live a simple life, we are choosing to see Him more clearly by getting rid of the distraction of thousands of objects.

Minimalism doesn't just apply to things; it also applies to our time and what we think about. Take a deep breath and imagine you're standing in the shade of a beautiful forest. The temperature is perfect, the air is crisp, and you feel perfectly at peace. We want to create a life that is full of more moments that feel like this. The only way we can accomplish this is by saying no to the stress and anxiety of keeping up with the Joneses both in possessions and in lifestyle.

Decluttering

While embracing minimalism often includes decluttering, they are not the same thing. To declutter something is a one-time action. We go through an area of our home, and we pare down the stuff in that area. To be honest, you could declutter a space and simply relocate the excess stuff to another room. While you did indeed declutter the kitchen counter, you have not gotten rid of anything.

You may also declutter in a huge way because of a major life change (i.e., you're moving, you're cleaning out a parent's house, you're adding another child to your family, etc.) Getting rid of things, for this reason, does not mean you're going to be a minimalist. You may simply move to another home and fill it up again. Decluttering is an action. You can take this action over and over again. It's a great action to take, but it doesn't mean you're embracing a minimalist lifestyle.

Organization

Organizing our stuff can often feel like decluttering or minimalism. We take a very messy space, we put everything into neat storage containers with labels and suddenly the space feels so much lighter. We look at it with pride! While I commend you on your organizational skills, if you did not get rid of anything, this can hardly be considered decluttering or minimalism.

Organizing is the way we keep our things, it is not about the philosophy of whether or not we should keep them in the first place. I believe it is important to first embrace the philosophy of minimalism, then go through and declutter your home and then finally to set about organizing what is left.

Organizing is fun! Don't think I'm knocking the great satisfaction of perfectly organizing a space. But clearly you can organize your 200 beanie bears and your 75 pieces of makeup, and this has nothing to do with minimalism or decluttering.

As you continue reading this book and diving into minimalism, keep in mind the difference between these three terms. Ask yourself which one you're embracing at the moment. They each have their place in helping you to create a peaceful, domestic church but understanding which one to use at which moment is important for your success!

The Process: Steps to a Minimalist Lifestyle

CHAPTER 11:
BE PREPARED

I feel giddy as I start this section! I love beginning new projects. I love planning and lists and starting new adventures! Let it be known that I enjoy planning far more than executing or finishing. My hope is that by making this process simple and straightforward, I can motivate you (and myself) to make it to the finish line!

Identify the People Involved

Are you going to do this on your own? Do you need to involve your spouse or your children? Do they need to be involved in every decision or just their personal belongings?

You have to decide if you want to be (or perhaps need to be) the leader of this Minimalism Adventure or if others need to be invited into the planning process. If you will be doing this as a team, I recommend scheduling a planning meeting with cookies and a specific end time. Many people don't want to sign up for a meeting that could take 2 hours. Keep it short and sweet!

Either print off worksheets ahead of time or if you're not sure which ones you'll need, have a laptop/computer handy to print them off once your family decides which ones you'll need.

Choose A Timeline

First things first, you must choose a timeline. Some of you will want to go through your house start to finish in as many days as it takes you to tackle every room. Some of you will prefer to work more slowly, perhaps a little each day or a certain block of time each weekend.

On the following pages are some examples of timelines you can choose from. Pick a timeline that's good for your personality and the lifestyle of your family. If you want to participate in the 8-Week Challenge with Sterling, visit www.sterlingjaquith.com/minimalism for more details!

The 8-Week Challenge

This is my preference for tackling my own home mostly because I can do it during Lent or start in the Fall before Advent. Lent is a wonderful time to make sacrifices and to draw closer to the Lord. September is the start of my favorite season and since I like to think of Advent as the Catholic New Year, I enjoy doing my big declutter-a-thon starting in September and ending right before Advent so I can focus on having a quiet season of preparation for Christmas.

Planning your life around the Liturgical calendar is deeply satisfying. I believe it's what our soul really craves. When we make Christ the anchor of the minimalist process, He becomes the lens through which we look through to decide what to fill our homes with. As we aim to grow closer to Him, we loosen the bonds that the world has on us. Below are the themes for each week that I recommend for the 8-week challenge.

Week One: Bedroom
Clothes, shoes, accessories, piles, storage, etc.
Week Two: Bathrooms
Toiletries, drawers, cleaning supplies, towels, etc.
Week Three: Kitchen
Refrigerator, pantry, junk drawer, cabinets, etc.
Week Four: Kid's Rooms
Clothes, books, toys, linens, blankets, etc.
Week Five: Garage
Tools, Totes, Lawn Care, Stored Decorations, etc.
Week Six: Office/School Room
Mail/Email, Documents, Books, Supplies, Curriculum, etc.
Week Seven: Living Room (and Catch Up)
Books, Pillows, Piles, Decoration, Storage, etc.
Week Eight: Your Mind
Positive Thoughts, Be A Scientist, Moving Forward, etc.

The 30-Day (or 40-Day) Challenge

There are many websites online that will lead you through a 30 or 40-day challenge. Simply Google "30-day declutter challenge" and you'll find many resources. This is a great option if you want to stay focused for a month or so moving through each room in your home.

The Marathoner

You want to dive in and not come up for air until the whole house is finished! For those of you with small houses or persistent personalities, this could be a good option for you. You might be able to do this after three hardcore days of decluttering. Others might need a solid week.

I want to caution against burnout. Many people, myself included, WANT to do this but lose steam before the job is done leaving piles around the house, creating more mess than before. I still believe this is the best option for some of you, especially if your whole family is committed to slamming this out together! You can follow the 8-week program without holding yourself to the timeline. Simply move through each room until it's finished!

The Daily Doer

You are committed to working on this project every day. Whether you're going to set aside a small amount of time each day or several hours, you will set aside daily time to focus on minimalism. If you choose this timeline, you can either commit to spending time on this every day (excluding Sundays) indefinitely, or you can set a deadline for your work to be ultimately finished (i.e., three months, one year, etc.) You can follow the 8-week program without holding yourself to that timeline. Simply move through each room at your own pace.

The Weekend Warrior

Choose a certain time block that you will focus on minimalism each weekend until you have gone through every item you own. How many hours will you dedicate to this work? Will you tackle this on Saturday only or will you choose to spend part of Sunday doing this as well?

In general, I'm a fan of taking Sundays off for rest, however, some people have unique work schedules and Sunday is not their official day of rest. For some of you, taking an entire weekend to slam out most of your house is the best way for you to get this done. As long as you don't make it a habit of working on Sunday, I think you can do this once or twice to accomplish the goal of embracing minimalism in your home and with your family.

The Specific Scheduler

Some of you have very busy schedules and you know you'll need to carve out specific time for this job. You may need to create blocks of time in your calendar on various dates working around the appointments you already have. Sit down and get these minimalism sessions on your calendar. Schedule at least one hour per session. I would schedule at least 4 hours of total time. Then I would reflect on what I was able to get done in that time to determine how much more time I would need in the future.

The Task Master

Some of you are already feeling overwhelmed. You need to dip your toes in… you need baby steps. Instead of staring at your entire home as the project, you're going to focus on a few very specific tasks first. You will pick something small to start with like your shoes or your gardening tools.

I have a list of suggested tasks on my website for The Task Master. You may start out as a Task Master and find that the process is not as scary as you thought. If this is the case, I suggest you pause and choose a separate timeline to keep yourself accountable to.

Choose The Order of Your Work

Next, you need to choose which rooms you will work on and put them in order. You might choose to weave through your home in the order that the rooms exist. I have given you a specific order for the 8-Week Challenge. Feel free to use that or to use the worksheet I've provided on my website to plan your own room order.

I think it's great to start with your bedroom first, specifically starting with your clothes. By tackling your own personal items first, you don't need to involve anyone else and this shows your commitment to getting rid of your own things before asking anyone else to make sacrifices. This also tends to be a common area where our stuff is out of control, so it feels great to purge!

You could group like-rooms together (i.e. we'll all start with bedrooms, then move on to common rooms.)

You could pick the order based on the schedules of people involved (i.e. Mom will do the kitchen Saturday morning while dad takes Tim to his baseball game. Dad and Tim will tackle the garage Saturday evening.)

Whatever your reasoning, commit to an order and write it down.

Prepare Staging Areas

Next, you need a plan for what to do with all the stuff you're going through! Here are the categories I use to stage my stuff. You can choose how you want to stage your stuff (i.e. pile on the floor, a bag, a box, a trash can, etc.) You certainly don't need to utilize all these categories!

Keep

Find a permanent home for all the things you want to keep right away if it's going to stay in the room. For example, if you're working on your closet, choose where shoes will live permanently and then put the shoes you're going to keep there as you're sorting.

Relocate

These are things you're going to keep, but they won't have a permanent home in the room you're working on. It can be tempting to take it to the right room as soon as you put your hands on the item. Resist this urge! Consolidate trips to other rooms by putting items in this pile.

Trash/Recycle

You can choose to keep your trash and recycling items together and separate them out later, or you can have one place for each of these categories. If I know I'm going to be dealing with a lot of cardboard or paper, I will have a bag or a box specifically for recycling.

Donate

For items you don't want to keep, consider donating it to your local St. Vincent de Paul or a family in need that you can visit directly.

Sell

Do not underestimate the money to be made from garage sales and Craigslist! You can get good money for used items!

Return

Make a pile of things that belong to friends/family that you need to return. I have a permanent place in my house for this category.

Tips For Success

After your planning session, print off the Tips For Success handout and make sure you read these before you begin!

Take a Before Picture

Take a picture on your phone or your digital camera. You may feel embarrassed now, but you'll be so proud of the work you've done, you'll want to share your progress with others! You will regret not doing this!

Drink Water

Have some water available preferably in a water bottle, so you don't risk knocking over a glass while you're working and creating more of a mess! Some of you might be tempted to live off coffee, and Diet Coke...don't do it! You're running a marathon here, and your body needs good old fashioned water. Don't let a dehydration headache steal your mojo.

Choose Some Tunes

Load up some inspirational music whether that's worship music, Gregorian chant or Taylor Swift. Pick something that will energize you!

Take Notes

Keep your Getting It Done worksheet handy with a pen so you can take notes while you're working! Here you will write down notes about what containers you need to store things more effectively. I also take notes about things I need to reorder and on what schedule (i.e. toilet paper once per month, fire alarm batteries once per year, etc.) These notes are going to help you run your home smoothly in the future!

Set A Timer

If you're anything like me, you get so excited about something that you want to dive in and not come up for air until it's finished and perfect! Unfortunately, that's rarely a good strategy for our bodies or our attention span. I suggest you set a timer for 50 minutes. Be focused for that time and then take a 10-minute break. Go outside, grab a healthy snack, make a phone call... switch gears so your brain gets a break. Then if you've planned to work longer, dive back in for another 50 minutes.

CHAPTER 12:
THE "GETTING IT DONE" WORKSHEET

After you are all prepared and have chosen your timeline for minimalizing your home, the next thing to do is to print off a Getting It Done worksheet before you're ready to tackle an area or room of your home. You can either print off a generic Getting It Done worksheet or you can print off a room/area specific one.

The purpose of this worksheet is to take notes along the way, so you don't forget anything. I want you to remember any major changes you made, and tasks that you think of while you're going through the room, anything you need to purchase, or anything that comes to mind that you want to jot down for reference later.

On the following pages you'll find the components that you'll find on every Getting It Done worksheet:

Storage Solutions Needed

As you're moving things around, what storage tools do you want? Be very specific. If you have a measurement in mind, write that down. This can include anything from totes, drawer organizers, hangers, hooks on the wall, bins under the bed, small boxes, etc.

Items to be Replaced or Fixed

If something is broken or needs to be replaced, write it down in this section. Be specific, so it's easier for you to take action later.

Relocated

We just recently decided to put diapers in the bathroom instead of the girls' bedroom. This was a major change, and so I wrote that down. I made sure later to tell everyone in the family, "The diapers have a new home in the bathroom." This will help you remember anything that used to live in this room but is now going to be relocated to another room.

Tasks That Need to be Scheduled

As you're going through the room, write down any tasks you need to schedule. Examples include order more toilet paper, change the air filter, schedule a play date with Stacy so I can return her book, etc.

Lots of things will pop into your mind as you're decluttering your space. Don't let them derail you. Simply write down the task and take care of it later. Don't fall for productive procrastination!

General Notes

I have a very poor memory. If I don't write something down, I genuinely think I will remember it, but I really won't. This section is for anything else that comes to mind.

Room Specific Worksheet

The two additions to a room specific worksheet are questions to ask and then the specific examples of things to get rid of. I call this section the Challenge Yourself section. These are just common problem areas that many people have related to this type of space in a home.

CHAPTER 13:
THE MINIMALISM TEST
SHOULD IT STAY OR SHOULD IT GO?

True happiness is to rejoice in the truth, for to rejoice in the truth is to rejoice in You, O God, who are the truth. Those who think that there is another kind of happiness look for joy elsewhere, but theirs is not true joy. - - Saint Augustine

Your goal should be to touch every single thing you own and determine if you want to keep it or not. You are now choosing to live intentionally and that means knowing what you have and purposefully deciding whether it will serve you in the future or not.

Everything must pass two tests to remain in the home. First, it must go through the Faith Test and then it must go through the Life Test. The Faith Test is a series of five questions that help determine whether an item is helping you strive for sainthood. Is this thing helping you serve God, your family, your community, or yourself as God wants you to be?

Next, it must pass the Life Test. The questions in the Life Test are related to whether something is practical, necessary, or sentimental. These two sets of questions will help you determine if something stays or goes. These are also the questions I use to determine if I'm going to purchase something.

The Danger of Joy

You have probably heard the phrase "Love is not a feeling, it's a choice." This applies to the word joy as well. We often think of joy as the warm, tingly, bubbly sensation we experience when we're having fun or bursting with excitement. While we may experience those feelings when something wonderful happens, this is not the only way to experience joy.

Being joyful is more a state of mind. It's a choice to be grateful… to be content with what we have and what we're doing. We can choose joy in the worst of circumstances by giving praise to God for what we do have and because He loves us.

> *"Joy does not simply happen to us.*
> *We have to choose joy and keep choosing it every day."*
> Fr. Henri Nouwen

In *The Magical Art of Tidying* up by Kon Mari[ix], the author urges people to touch each possession they own and ask the question, "Does this spark joy?" While I agree with the heart of what this question is trying to get at (does this item really have value to you?), the question is misleading. If we think of joy as warm, bubbly feelings… it's unlikely we will find value in our toothbrush or our toilet cleaner.

Instead, I suggest we first ask ourselves four questions related to the Lord to determine whether or not something finds a place in our home or gets tossed in the trash/giveaway box. All these questions come down to love.

Let us make the purpose of what we own be to help us, love. I believe that is how Jesus would look at all possessions. Is this helping me spread love in the world? Each item we keep should serve one of the four categories on the next page.

Faith Test

Does this item help me love the Lord?

There are many religious items in our house that we use, maybe only once a year, to show our love to the Lord. Catholic traditions and living liturgically are beautiful ways we can express our faith. I don't view the candles, prayer books, or liturgical decorations that we own as frivolous.

Danger: If you collect so many religious items that your home becomes cluttered with them and your family loses peace over cleaning, organizing, and managing these things, perhaps you have gone overboard. Don't use the noble excuse of practicing your faith as a reason to hoard religious stuff.

Does this item help me love myself as God created me?

A toothbrush keeps your teeth clean. It probably doesn't spark joy but we can find a deep satisfaction in taking care of our body - the earthly temple God has given us.

Danger: When we cross the line from taking care of ourselves and looking presentable, we can find ourselves succumbing to vanity and pride. We can practice cleanliness and modest dressing without giving into buying all the latest and greatest creams or cramming our closet with clothing options.

Does using this item help me love my family?

The Lord calls us to love and care for our family starting first with our immediate family and then our extended family. Some items in your home will be directly related to spending quality time with your family. If you have six children, it's likely you will also own six bicycles and six helmets. While these things do take up space and aren't strictly necessary for living, they promote a healthy lifestyle and a free way to spend quality time together.

Danger: If you lean too heavily on buying kid's toys or activity toys (i.e., bikes, kayaks, camping gear, ski equipment, etc.,) you might be stressed trying to earn enough money to maintain and store all these things. Are you really using these tools to grow closer to your family or are you chasing a dream life that in reality is just accumulating dust in your garage?

Does using this item help me love people in my community?

There are several items in my kitchen that we only use when hosting large groups of people. We do this often, and when I look at these items, I see the love we are able to spread by hosting other families in our home. Community is important.

Danger: It's easy to want to serve others but let that attitude turn into wanting to impress others. Your guests don't care if you serve them fancy food or have beautiful china. They seek your company and your friendship. Don't use community events as an excuse to bedazzle your home just to "make others feel more comfortable."

Does the beauty of this item draw me and others closer to God?

Arthur Lohsen of the Catholic News Agency explains, "Beauty is the single aspect of God which can be expressed physically within the earthly realm. Beauty is not merely Man's arrogance or a waste of resources which could be directed to the poor. Beautiful settings, artwork, music, and liturgy are appropriate and necessary aspects of God's everlasting mystical presence before Mankind."[x]

Beauty is real and surrounding ourselves with items that remind us of the beauty of the Kingdom of God is a good thing. Ask yourself honestly whether the items in your home have the type of beauty that points you to the Lord.

Danger: It can be tempting to keep everything that is remotely attractive to look at and give the excuse of being drawn to God as a reason for keeping it. Not everything that is pleasing to look at is truly beautiful and reminds us of Heaven and the goodness of God.

Let's use these questions as a Catholic guide to minimalism. Our lives should be dedicated to know, love and serve God. It makes sense that what we keep in our homes should be in service of that mission as well.

Life Test

The following questions are ones you'll find in most minimalist books and articles. These tend to be more practical questions about whether you need an item or whether you're holding on to it for an emotional reason. That is not to say we cannot keep things simply for sentimental value but it's important to be intentional.

You may choose to ask yourself some or all of these questions. There will also be room specific questions listed on the room specific Getting It Done worksheets. These are just guides. If you're a professional artist, you're going to keep a lot more art supplies than someone who is a car mechanic. There are no right and wrong choices when it comes to practicing minimalism.

The guiding principle should always be intentionality. Are you going to keep this for a specific reason and are you okay with that? Would you feel comfortable sharing that reason with your spouse and friends? Here's what you can ask to put something through the Life Test:

Do you love it? Do you need it? Do you want it?

Do you have room to store it?

Has this item been used in the last year?

Does this belong to your fantasy self?

Can someone else make better use of it?

If you were out shopping today, would you purchase this item?

Does this item have sentimental value?

Is this a stand-in for a memory?

Do you have/need more than one of this item?

Will something similar that you have get the job done?

Is it broken? Are you actually going to fix it? If so, when?

Does this item fit you, your home, and your current lifestyle?

Do you have a realistic plan to use this in the near future?

Is this the best room for it?

How long do you need to keep it? When can you get rid of it?

Can you borrow or purchase another one if needed?

Can you return it?

Can it be digitized?

Would you rather have the space that this takes up?

If you want to simplify this process, you can ask yourself, "Does this item add value to my life?" Then do that over and over and over again—with everything you own. Constantly. Habitually.xi The next chapters of the book will feature room specific questions to consider on your minimalism journey!

CHAPTER 14:
ROOM SPECIFIC GUIDES

In this section, I will guide you through each area of your home by posing questions to help you be more intentional about your decisions. These questions are simply to be used as a guide to help get your creative juices flowing and to challenge you as to what role Christ is playing in each room. There are also some specific categories covered in the third section of this book including sentimental items and decorations.

In addition to these room specific questions, the Getting It Done worksheets also feature specific ideas for what to get rid of with check boxes to motivate you to challenge yourself about common problem areas. If you want to be more or less extreme in what you choose to keep in each room, go for it – it's your home! **Resources at www.sterlingjaquith.com/minimalism**

Your Clothing, Shoes, and Accessories

I want to start with this category because I believe it's the easiest to tackle and often the most satisfying. It's also the best place to start because you don't need to consult anyone else. They are your clothes so you can decide what you keep and what to toss. You may even win some good will with your spouse and family by starting here.

Many websites suggest that you empty your entire closet before beginning. If I had a small closet, I would definitely do this. Because my current closet houses a lot of stuff that isn't clothing, I don't empty the entire space. Instead, I pull out all my clothes, shoes, and accessories and lay them out on my bed.

Capsule Wardrobe

This is a term that has become trendy as of late. It's the idea that you have a small number of items to wear and that most of these items go with each other. For example, you don't have a pair of bright yellow pants that really only go with a bright magenta t-shirt that you can really only wear to a beach party in the summer. Instead, you choose colors and styles that go together. Some people have a capsule wardrobe for different seasons.

I found that the idea of a capsule wardrobe was very appealing, but it was hard to pull off when we had a small family. When my husband and I just had one or two children, we didn't do laundry all that often. Now that we have four children, we do a load of laundry every other day. This means I can have less clothing because I know it's going to get washed quickly. This is true for my kid's clothes as well!

Now my wardrobe is mostly cool colors (dusty rose pink, cream, gray, steel blue, etc.) Most of my wardrobe goes together so I don't have to think much about putting together outfits. Most of my outfits now go with the three pairs of shoes I like to wear every day.

My children's clothes also follow a capsule wardrobe outline. Their clothes are mostly pink, purple, and teal. I am particular about the shades of pink and purple to make sure any item of clothing can be paired with anything else. This has also cut down on the number of conversations I have with them about their clothes since I don't have to say, "That shirt doesn't go with those pants" anymore.

If you're interested in learning more about this idea, read about the challenge to wear only 33 items for three months at www.bemorewithless.com/project-333/.

Tips Before You Begin

- Be prepared to try everything on.

- Remind yourself why you're doing this. Close your eyes and envision what a clean and clear closet looks like and how easy it is to keep your clothing organized.

- Consider enlisting the help of a friend to keep you strong!

Questions To Ask About Each Item

These are the questions I ask myself in the order in which I ask them, so my decision-making process is as easy as possible. The order is important because if something is broken, I don't even bother to ask myself if I like it or if it fits.

1. Is it smelly, stained or in disrepair? Am I going to fix that?

   I almost never repair clothing or even attempt to get stains out of them. I will run clothes through a super-hot laundry cycle to get a smell out of them. Know yourself and what you're willing to do. If you will never sew on that missing button, get rid of the item.

2. Does this style of clothing match the image I want to project?

   I have very different requirements for clothes I wear at home, clothes I wear out, and clothes I wear to speaking engagements. I know what purpose each piece of clothing has so I can ask myself if it projects the image I want in each situation.

Do I feel comfortable getting housework done in my house clothes? Do I feel confident wearing my street clothes? Do I feel polished and professional in my speaking clothes?

Sometimes my clothes are notably out of fashion. It's obvious I bought that item in the early 2,000's, and that's why I never wear it. Most of the time, I buy clothes that are classic and fairly timeless. Other times I buy clothes for comfort, and I don't care if they're fashionable or not.

3. Do I actually wear it? Am I comfortable when I wear it?

   If I don't wear something, I really press myself about why. Do I always have to iron it before or dry clean it after so I avoid wearing it? Is it itchy, scratchy, or uncomfortable?

   Our actions speak louder than our intentions. If I consistently pass up a piece of clothing, eventually I have to admit that for whatever reason, I'm not wearing it and it may be time to let it go.

4. Is it a great statement piece that I rarely take out?

   I have a few stunning dresses that are too loud to wear all the time, so I'm always waiting for just the right moment to pull them out. Alas, has it been three years since I've found that moment? Even if I adore the dress and I know it'd be a showstopper, if that opportunity so rarely presents itself that it simply hangs in my closet for months, perhaps it's not worth holding onto it.

Now, there are some clothes I wear a few times per year, and I'm okay with that. I have a red dress that I wear around Christmas and on Pentecost. I'm okay that I pull it out seasonally. I also have a purple dress I like to wear for Lent and Advent. To me, these are good reasons to keep something you don't wear often, but I do wear them all at least once per year.

5. Does it fit?

    This is the last question I ask myself because I often keep things that don't fit. Since I am often pregnant, postpartum, or losing weight after having a baby, I will actually wear these things again. If a piece of clothing has made it through the other questions and if I believe I'll wear it again when I'm that size again, I keep it.

    If it's a size 4 and I've never managed to be a size 4 or I was a size 4 for three days in the summer of 2008, then it's probably time to admit, I won't be wearing it anytime soon.

Bonus Question: Would I buy this again right now?

Sometimes I like this question. It's thought provoking, and it helps me decide whether or not to keep something. Sometimes I loathe this question because I have no money and it stresses me out to think about whether or not I could buy this (or anything) and then I spiral into sadness about my current situation. Know yourself and whether or not you want to consider this while you're going through your closet.

Shoes

Some people have a serious shoe problem. Others, like my sister-in-law, have a few pair of shoes and they don't struggle in this area at all. Her self-control is amazing!

First, be honest about who you are. Is this a problem area for you? Are you emotionally attached to shoes? Do you have a shoe problem? By being honest about this up front, it will help you tackle your problem with more grace and humility.

I used to put a lot more stock in wearing the perfect shoe to each event. Now that I'm running after kids all day, I find that I need far fewer shoes. I've gotten rid of most of my fancy or "cool" shoes in favor of more utilitarian shoes like hiking boots, fall time boots, water shoes, and a good sneaker to wear throughout the day.

I also have almost all flat shoes. I'm a big fan of ballet flats. They are good "mom" shoes that make you look polished but also allow you to chase after a toddler. Gone are the days when I used to wear heels often. I finally pared my high heel shoe collection down to four, and there are some days I even consider that to be excessive.

On the following page are the questions you can ask about each of the pair of shoes that you own.

Questions To Ask About Pair of Shoes

There's just one question you need to ask yourself honestly: do you really need this pair of shoes? If you need a little more guidance though, on the follow page are some more questions to ask!

Do they fit?

Do they need to be repaired?

Do I have more than one shoe for the same purpose (i.e. three tennis shoes)

When is the last time I wore these shoes?

Do these shoes give me blisters?

Are these shoes uncomfortable?

Are they still in style?

Could you give them to someone in need?

Are you setting a good example for your children?

If you're too embarrassed to count up every single pair of shoes you have and post that number on your Facebook status... you probably have too many shoes.

Accessories

Accessories are not a particular weakness of mine. In fact, I tend to wear no accessories at all. I admire others who can pull off the perfect statement necklace or who know how to artfully tie a scarf. Those touches can really make an outfit sing! Perhaps there will be a different time in my life when I pay more attention to these little details but for now, since I don't, I have tossed almost all of my accessories.

I have two scarves, some jewelry, some headbands, and one belt. This makes sense for me because I don't wear many accessories. If you are an accessories queen, the questions are about the same as the clothing and shoe questions.

Questions To Ask Accessories

Do I wear it?

Does it match the clothes I wear?

Am I keeping it for sentimental reasons (read the Sentimental Chapter)

Is it broken, stained, or rusted?

How many belts, scarves, gloves, hats, etc. do I really need?

Can I sell this and buy something I would enjoy more?

Can someone in need use this?

Can I give this to a friend or family member?

Master Bedroom

After tackling your clothing, both in your drawers and in your closet, it's time to move on to the rest of your bedroom. Your bedroom should be a place of peace. It should be a safe haven for you to come and relax. If you're married, it should be a place for you to connect with your spouse.

We tend to want to wake up to a clean kitchen, but I think it's just as crucial to wake up to a tidy bedroom. After all, it's the last place you see at night and the first place you see in the morning. Your bedroom should not be a dumping ground for all the miscellaneous things that pop up during the day. Trust me; I know how tempting it is to do that.

Involve Your Spouse

If you are married, acknowledge that this space belongs to you and your spouse. If they want nothing to do with your minimalism/decluttering/redecorating projects then maybe you can skip this part. Even if, on the other hand, your husband proclaims not to care, be careful. He might not appreciate you chucking one-third of his stuff and decorating everything in bright florals. If you're going to make major changes, either make them together or at least review them with your spouse so it's not a huge surprise.

Decide The Room's Purpose

I recommend setting up your bedroom so that all you do there is sleep and relax, if possible. If it needs to be a space that has multiple uses, create some boundary conditions on when the space is used for each activity.

For example, my bedroom now has a computer in it so I can

do work when the baby is sleeping. To create a boundary, I try not to work at all in my bedroom during the evening. I turn my computer completely off so it doesn't cause me any anxiety when I'm in bed (or wake me up with 3 AM windows updates).

Focus on Beauty

Art

When it comes to designing your domestic church, art work is a very important aspect that sets the tone for each space. This is especially important in your bedroom. Design your bedroom so it points to Christ. Make sure to have some religious artwork or inspiring quotes around.

Above our bed I hung a beautiful black and white print of my husband and me on our wedding day. It's such a good reminder of the promises we made on our wedding day and helps me to be humble and charitable when I don't feel like it!

Bed Spread

Choose sheets and a blanket (or duvet cover) that makes you smile. We have one nice set of sheets for the summer and one nice set of sheets for the winter. I chose a simple white blanket to go on our bed. I love how the white makes the room feel more simple and romantic. It didn't cost that much money, but it has greatly improved how I feel when I walk into my bedroom.

I also make our bed every day so the place has a nice tidy, finished feel to it. This is easy for me to do since we have no throw pillows. I simply tug the blankets up to the top!

Little Touches

If you love flowers, consider getting a vase with some real or fake flowers. This can really brighten a space. Use trays and bowls to hold the little things you leave on your dresser or nightstand (i.e. keys, jewelry, change, etc.) This will make those piles feel intentional. You can get cheap decorative bowls and trays at a thrift store.

Maximize Storage

Books

There are several ways to better organize the stuff that lives in your bedroom. I believe book shelves or book cases are pretty essential in just about every room. It's likely you will accumulate books in your bedroom so make sure you have a place for them, even if it's a small shelf.

Night Stands

I recommend using a dresser in place of a nightstand. By using a dresser, you will have more surface area to place the things beside your bed. A dresser will also have drawers instead of just being a tiny table like most nightstands are.

Under The Bed

Use the space under your bed for storage. Anything that can be put out of sight will help your home feel more peaceful and free from clutter overload! This also helps keep things from getting trapped under the bed since the space is being used for something else. Storing wrapping supplies or seasonal clothes under the bed is a good use of that space!

Minimalism is not just about cleaning up a space. It's about intentionally creating an atmosphere of peace in each room of your home. You spend a great deal of time in your bedroom, even if it's only to sleep! Create a space that helps you unplug, connect with your spouse, and draw closer to the Lord.

Master Bedroom Questions

Do I have a theme or a color scheme to the room?

Do I like the art on the walls?

How many blankets/sheets do I have?

Where can I maximize storage?

What am I keeping on the night stand?

Where do books go?

Where do I throw my clothes at the end of the night?

What piles tend to appear in my room? Where can they go instead?

Can I get rid of the TV?

Bathrooms

Next up, tackle the bathrooms. I find that bathrooms are also not very emotional to minimalize. Since it's such a utilitarian space, it's easy and fast to sort through what stays and what goes. Truthfully, cleaning bathrooms is a lot harder than decluttering them, and some of us desperately need to deep clean our bathrooms!

The secret to an intentional bathroom is that it's tidy enough to get in and get out with ease and also easy to clean. If there are so many hair clips, towels, and eye shadow boxes laying around that it's difficult to find what you need (or to reach and use cleaning supplies), your bathroom is going to steal your peace.

Start by keeping only the essentials and then come up with a plan for cleaning the bathroom on a regular basis, so it feels light and fresh instead of dingy and grimy.

Tips Before You Begin

- Print off some accessories worksheets if you need them.
- Decide if you're going to do all bathrooms in one day.
- Involve other bathroom users.
- Layout all hair accessories and makeup on the counter.
- Group like-items together. Organization is key in bathrooms!

Personal Care Items

This section is all about hair accessories, oral hygiene items, shower/bath tools, toilet paper, etc. This may look overwhelming but going through these items goes fast!

Grab a towel or a blanket and lay it out on a counter, a nearby bed, or the floor. Dump ALL your bathroom stuff here so you can see it all at once. Immediately go through and get rid of trash.

Next, create piles of like items (i.e., hair stuff, makeup, bath items, etc.) Do a quick pass and toss things that you obviously don't want or need. I find that at least one-fourth can be discarded without getting your emotions involved.

Now comes the tricky part. Now you need to be more discerning.

Towels and Linens

Bathrooms often have towels and may even have linens stored in a closet or on some shelving. The key to being intentional about these items is to ask yourself, "How often do I really use these?" Could you get away with storing half away and only using two towels in rotation?

That's it for this section. Can you live with less? This will be easier or harder depending on how often your household does laundry.

Medicine Cabinet

This section is also fast and simple. Ask the following questions about each item:

- Is it expired?

- Are there duplicates I can combine?

- Is this the right place to store this? (i.e., maybe band aids and other first aid materials should live somewhere else, or perhaps you've shoved bobby pins in here, and they should be somewhere else.)

- Do I actually use this?

Bathroom Questions

Do I have duplicate (or old) hygiene items (i.e., lotion, shampoo, tooth paste, etc.)

What makeup do I actually use?

Do I use all my styling tools (brushes, flat iron, curler, razors, etc.)?

Where should towels go? Can I get rid of some?

Is any medicine expired?

Where do cleaning products go? Do I have duplicates or old ones?

Do I need to keep those travel sized bottles?
How can I keep the counters mostly clear?

Cleaning System

Bathrooms can quickly spiral out of control because we tend to buzz through them quickly in a rush to get ready and out the door. We haphazardly toss our brushes and makeup about. I'd love to say if we just had the right system, we would clean the bathroom as we go. I know, however, for me personally, that would set me up for failure.

You're going to leave your bathroom a mess sometimes, and that's okay. What's important is that you don't let it stay that way for too long. It should really never be cluttered for more than one day, but just to be nice, let's give ourselves two days.

Pick two days per week that you tidy your bathroom. You can call it Tidy Tuesday and Tidy Thursday. Then do a full cleaning of your bathroom Saturday morning, so if you have company over the weekend, it's sparkling clean!

Alternatively, you can tidy on Monday and Wednesday with a full clean on Friday, which still sets you up for success if you have company over for the weekend.

Either of these schedules ensures that it never stays messy for more than two days.

In my house, we try to tidy the bathroom every evening before we go to bed. Sure, we miss a day here and there, but I've been working hard to ingrain this habit into the children… and myself!

We ask ourselves at the end of the day, "Is this space ready for the next person?" That means the items have been put away, any major goop has been cleaned off the counter and the toilet paper isn't empty.

Bathrooms are easy to tend to if you do a little bit every day or a few days per week. It's when we forget about them that they tend to build up gross and fuzzy things as well as counter spaces that get filled with clutter. You will need the help of your family members to keep this area of your house clean.

Toy Management

"If you want your children to turn out well,
spend twice as much time with them as half as much money."
—Abigail Van Buren[xii]

Before we dive into kid rooms, it's important to first discuss overall toy management. American kids have too many toys. You don't need me to convince you of this. You know it deep down or perhaps at least couch cushion deep. America has 3.1% of the world's children but buys 40% of the world's toys.[xiii] Yikes!

This has got to stop. We have to squash this idea that more plastic, noise making, colorful, exciting toys are going to make our children happy. We are robbing them of the truly important things: loving nature, experiencing the truly beautiful, expanding their imaginations, discovering God in the simple things.

Stop worrying about your mother-in-law's feelings. Yes, we are called to be kind to one another, but that doesn't mean we should allow family members to dump toys in our home without considering the consequences. There are many more ways we can help each other around the holidays than giving each other more stuff.

I talk about managing family relations during the holidays in my book *Be Merry* with some concrete ideas for how to handle these tricky conversations and requests.

Be intentional about what comes in your home. Protect your children. You are the adult. You are the parent. You are the one who controls how their childhood is shaped. My husband really appreciates that we don't keep too many toys around, so the kids are encouraged to play outside or be creative.

"One of the most valued goals my husband and I have in raising our herd is to guide their focus to the right things. By over-indulging them, we are doing them a disservice. Not only are kids who have a ton of toys less artistic, more overstimulated, and more likely to be materialistic adults, they're not very fun to be around." – Allie Casazza[xiv]

Toy Alternatives

Make a list of toy alternatives specific to your family that you want to focus on this year. Here are some ideas:

- Experiences (road trips, zoo pass, tickets to a sporting event or the theater, camping trip, etc.) If you're too busy to do these things, you're too busy. Spend quality time with your family. If you have no money, walks and picnics in the park are free!

- A skill or hobby (music, art, bow hunting, cooking lessons, etc.) Give your children something they will have for the rest of their life. They will be grateful for these skills.

- Supplies (art, music, woodworking, sewing, etc.) Help them get into a hobby or support one they already have.

- A board game and time to play with them

- Good books – you can never have too many books that are beautiful, virtuous, or inspiring

- Essentials (pajamas, shoes, clothing, water bottle, backpack, etc.) This is especially nice in large families where kids are often stuck with hand-me-downs and would love something of their own.

Once you have made this list, share it with your family before the holiday season. Explain that you're trying to minimize having buckets of toys and you'd like these instead. You can't force someone to give you what you want, but you can at least explain to them what you're trying to do as a family and hope that they'll join in!

Managing Toys

I'm not saying the kids shouldn't have any toys. Toys are fun and kids should get to enjoy toys. To help avoid the children (and you) feeling overwhelmed by toys, here are some suggestions from Kitty Lascurain at The Spruce.[xv]

Put Toys on Display

When kids can't see their toys, they don't play with them. Sick of your kids pulling out every last toy just to leave them lying all over the floor? Why not leave them out in the first place!

Instead of stuffing toys into baskets and bins, try organizing your little one's things into several themed play stations where toys remain largely on display. For instance, you might have a costume station with a hanging rack of dress-up clothes and a mirror, or a domestic play station with a toy kitchen and a basket of toy food. Set up a table with art supplies and building toys and a reading corner with a comfy chair and some books.

While it's important to allow creative cross play, you should encourage your children to clean up each station before moving to another. Your child will have a much easier time deciding what to play with, and you'll find it much easier to keep up with the mess.

Start a Toy Rotation

Playing with the same toys over and over again can get tiring after a while. Wondering how to keep your kiddos engaged? Try mixing things up a little!

A well-organized toy rotation helps to eliminate clutter while allowing children to play with a wider selection of toys. Since the available toys change on a regular basis, there is always something new and exciting to play with, ensuring your child will never get bored.

Worried your little one will miss their favorite things? There's nothing wrong with leaving a few toys, like Legos or a much-loved stuffed animal or doll, out on a permanent basis.

And if your kids are happy with the toys they currently have, it doesn't hurt to alter your rotation schedule. As long as your child is happy and engaged, there's no need to stress.

Make Books Interesting and Accessible

What's the point of having an extensive library of children's books if your kids never read them? Bookshelves are often difficult for little ones to access on their own, and with so many books to choose from, it's hard to know what to pick.

If you want to encourage your kids to read, try trading

traditional bookshelves for a few easy-to-access book rails. Book rails hold fewer books and display their covers better, making them more attractive to kids. Make sure your child can see and reach the books, and change the titles often to continually *peak* their interest. You can even make weekly trips to the library and have your kiddo choose and set up their own books!

Purchasing More Toys

You're going to purchase more toys in the future. You're going to receive more toys in the future. It's better to have a good plan of action than to be surprised when this happens.

When I'm getting ready to buy something for one of my kids, I first sit down and ask myself, "What did I buy them last year?" Quickly I realize that most of the time I don't remember, which emphasizes how superficial most toy purchases are. When I do remember, at least half the time, I realize the toy was a flop, and they weren't that interested in it after a few weeks. This is especially frustrating when I bought something that they fawned over at someone else's house. I'm getting better at avoiding the temptation to give into this type of purchase.

I also try to consider past purchases. If I can remember what Rose enjoyed when she was three, it helps me make better choices for Violet when she turns three. We've bought a lot of toys we mistakenly thought a child was ready for. I've learned a lot since then.

I keep saying I'm going to keep track of what I buy in a gifts journal but I've yet to do that. Perhaps I'll begin this year and encourage others to join me for extra accountability!

Once you've decided you are in fact going to buy more toys, identify the same size/type/number of pieces toy to get rid of. We have a one in, one out toy policy. This will also help you consider your purchase more carefully because it forces you to think, "Is this toy I'm bringing in going to provide more value than the one I'm getting rid of?"

You can do this! It may take baby steps, but you surely can reprogram your brain about toys. You can help your children understand that people and experiences are more important than things. You can raise children who don't fall prey to consumerism and materialism.

Kid Rooms

Moving on to kid rooms! Whether you have one child or twelve... whether you have little children or young adults... kid's rooms are always a vortex for stuff. Here's the hard truth: this is your fault.

Until kids have their own money and can drive, you are the one who enables them to bring things into the house. You have allowed the pileup of toys, books, papers, and clothes. In America, we are incredibly indulgent of kids having what they want and holding onto it for years. The good news is, you are also the person who can change this!

If you have older children, they can use the Master Bedroom worksheet and go through the minimalism process all on their own first before you review their room.

Prepare Them For Change

Before I dive into the how-to of going through kid rooms, I want to first talk about the philosophy of getting kids on board. Sometimes when parents get excited about a new lifestyle change, we expect the children to instantly hop on board without considering their feelings. Now as the parent, we do need to decide which direction our family ship is headed – but we can be mindful of our crew of little people in the process.

The older your kids are, the more ingrained their habits are. It will feel shocking if you suddenly say, "Get rid of most of your stuff right now, trust me it's better!" Instead, sit them down and explain what this whole minimalism thing is all about. It also helps if you've gone through your bedroom and closet first so you can lead them by example.

It's important to explain that we don't need a lot of things to make us happy and that having too many things means we can't spend time on the activities we truly enjoy (i.e. bike rides, playing games, reading, etc.) If we are always cleaning and organizing our things, we don't have as much free time. Children will understand this.

If you are worried that you're going to get a lot of push-back from your children, consider starting with half your goal in mind. If you have a picture in your mind of how much stuff you want them to have, consider letting them have twice that much (you'll still have to get rid of stuff to reach that goal) and then go through this process again in six months or a year.

You didn't end up living in a cluttered house overnight, and you don't need to fix it overnight either. Family peace and harmony are more important than the perfect idea of minimalism.

Set The Stage For Minimalism Day

Get them involved.

While it can be tempting to send the kids away for a few hours and do this yourself, you'll quickly find the room right back in disarray. The kids need to have buy-in. Not only should they be involved in what stays and what goes but they also need to understand the system of how to tidy going forward. Depending on attention span and maturity level, I involve kids between three and five years old.

NOTE: You know your own children. If you're drowning in toys and you know you're going to throw away more than half of what they have in their room, it might be better for you to do this alone. This is especially true for kids under ten. When they get back and challenge you about what you threw away, turn it around and ask them, "Well, what do you see is missing?" This will help them realize they probably weren't using all the toys, to begin with.[xvi]

Where should this live?

This is going to be the question you ask about each item in their room that stays. Everything must have a home, and your children must learn where that home is. They can help decide where things should go. Listen to their input as they are the ones who play with and use the stuff in their room. While going through this process, if you cannot find a place that makes sense for an item to live, consider tossing it or storing it in another part of the house.

Set a time limit.

This can drag on for hours, and your kids will lose heart. They may form a negative opinion of minimalism. Let them know how long you're going to tackle this project. I recommend 1-2 hours. If you have little kids, set a timer and take breaks every 10-15 minutes.

Provide an incentive and make it fun!

We try to make this process fun. We put music on. Give them water bottles like it's an event! Be cheery and positive. We act like it's an exciting thing to do. We also provide a reward at the end, either an experience like a family bike ride or a treat like ice cream. Try not to make the reward another toy! Avoid criticizing them. Remember that you as a family let it get to this place. It's not their fault.

Now that you've set the stage and gotten the family involved, it's time to tackle each kid room with gusto!

Kid Bedroom Questions

Do you use this?

Do you think we could give this to another child who has no toys?

Does this fit you?

Which do you like more X or Y?

Is this broken? Can we throw this away?

Would you like to mail that artwork to grandma?

Would you like to sell this at a garage sale?

Where should this live?

Cleaning System

Your kids will probably be tired and burnt out after the whole process so I would wait until the next day to go over a cleaning system. I bring my kids back to their room, and I name everything and point to its place.

- This is where your shoes live.

- This is where the dress-up clothes live.

- This is where dirty clothes live.

In my house, we often repeat this quote from Benjamin Franklin, "A place for everything and everything in its place." I say this with a cheery voice instead of a grating, nagging voice. Think of putting your Mary Poppins hat on for this! I'm certainly not that kind of mom all the time, but I want my kids to embrace minimalism before they leave my house as adults so I try to create positive associations with this process!

After showing them where everything lives, explain to them that this is what you want the room to look like when you ask them to clean their room. Especially if you have little children, consider taking a picture of each area and putting them on the wall as a reference point.

Since I know my children often forget to put everything away, I give them a warning and say, "Are you ready for the inspector to come inspect your room? Have you checked in all the sneaky places?" They inevitably realize they hadn't looked under the bed or on the couch and they do another quick pass before I come in to check.

Kitchen

Most people fall into two categories when it comes to decluttering the kitchen. Some are ridiculously excited to finally create some order in a place that they enjoy spending time. Others dread going through cabinets and drawers that have been stuffed to the brim for years. No matter which group you fall into, I promise you that by the end of reorganizing your kitchen, you will feel deeply satisfied and more willing to spend time cooking for your family.

I guarantee you have too much stuff in your kitchen. In the name of comfort and convenience, we have bought so many doodads to make our lives easier. In the end, we rarely use them and they make our kitchen feel dark and heavy instead of cheery and light. No wonder we don't want to spend time in such a space!

Full confession... I have successfully minimalized every room in my house, except the kitchen. Granted, it's a lot better than it was and every time I take a pass at it, I toss more stuff But trust me, I understand how hard this space is to pare down.

Give yourself some forgiveness. This area of your house may take the longest to get in order. You may make small progress here and there for a few years before it gets to where you want it. That's okay. We're fighting for a long-term lifestyle change here.

Involve All Cooks

This is also an area of the house where you can move far quickly if you work alone but that can be dangerous. Cooking is very personal, and God bless anyone in your family who helps out in the kitchen! Let's give them a voice. Whether it's your husband or an eager 10-year-old, anyone who cooks should at least be made aware of the Kitchen Minimalism project and allowed a voice to what's important to them before you go chucking things in the box marked Thrift Store!

Things You Probably Don't Need

After doing a lot of research on minimalist kitchens, most resources had the same "you don't need" list give or take a few items. This tells me that most of us don't need these things but we've been trained to buy and keep them anyway. Take a deep breath and really consider whether or not you need the following:

Stand Mixer

Few of us use our stand mixers if we're blessed enough to have one. Most of us can get away with mixing by hand, or a hand held blender. Unless you're a huge bread baker, you can probably skip buying this or let the one you have go.

Knife Sets

I'm not sure who started the trend of needing a knife set in a wooden block. It's bulky and unnecessary. Get one or two sharp knives and store them in a drawer or on a magnet strip against the wall.

Wok

C'mon, how often are you making Asian food that tastes significantly different from having been expertly cooked in your wok? Let it go. Using a regular pan is good enough.

Excessive Plates, Glasses, and Bowls

Get a set of 8 plates, glasses, and bowls. If you have a family of 10 or 12, get that many. You don't need more for hosting guests. You can buy fancy yet disposable plates at Target for the times you're hosting a huge party. Don't let annual hospitality dictate what lives in your house all year long. We have a cheap set from Ikea that was $30 for adults and a smaller set of plastic kid plates and cups that was also very inexpensive.

Multiple Sizes of Wine Glasses

Gasp! Can you put red wine and white wine in the same glass? Yes, one size can work for all. No, this isn't exactly proper or classy, but few of us live lives that necessitate multiple levels of stemware.

Machines For One Purpose

Ice cream maker, bread machine, rice cooker, pasta maker, toasted sandwich press, toaster, espresso machine, griddle, a juicer, etc. This is a personal choice. Perhaps you do use your rice cooker all the time. If so, keep it. But be honest with yourself. If you have a single purpose machine that's taking up space that you rarely use, consider letting it go to create more space in your kitchen and more freedom in your heart!

Specialty Baking Pans

Doughnut pans, paella pans, ramekins, animal shaped cake tins, springform cake tin, heart shaped tart tin, etc.

Oven Mitts

Food blogger Jules says, "Oven mitts are for sissies. Use a tea towel!"[xvii]

Single Use Utensils

Apple corer, egg slicer, lemon juicer, milk frother, etc. Again, these tools do make life easier but at what cost? How many trinkets do you need taking up space in your drawers and cupboards? Keep what you use, toss the rest.

Electric Carving Knife

Does anyone still have these? If you do, toss it out with your VHS's.

Kitchen Blowtorch

I'm sure your crème Brulee is on point when you make it but when was the last time you did? Enough said.

Exceptions! If you really do use something daily or weekly, consider keeping it. I froth my coffee every morning, and we make rice every week. We also make all our own coconut milk ice cream to save money, so we have a nice ice cream maker that we use plenty to justify keeping it. I also can't seem to part with my air popcorn maker, and we use it almost every Sunday for family movie night!

Stretch goal: no microwave! Did you know you can live without a microwave? I know, it sounds crazy! Plenty of families heat up their food on the stove. This helps you avoid convenience foods. Wellness Mama who is Catholic and has six kids doesn't own a microwave! I'm not there yet, but it's definitely one of my family goals within the next few years!

The Refrigerator/Freezer

I don't have much to add here because the same minimalism principles we've been talking about apply. Clear it out, clean it, then only put back what you use. Do this at least once every three months. I tend to do it right before a major feast (i.e., Easter, Christmas, Fourth of July, Thanksgiving, etc.)

Real Food, Real Time

My family tries to eat healthy food. For us, that means mostly meats, fruits, and veggies. We do very little sugar, dairy, or gluten. And you know what... this takes time. I try hard to pick recipes that are simple and easy, but I will never be able to beat cereal for breakfast or hot pockets for lunch when it comes to ease and timeliness.

A lot of the kitchen things we keep around are designed to save us time, but minimalism is about intentionality. Where do you want to spend your time? I'm not telling you it should be in the kitchen. You need to decide for yourself what's important and where you and your family want to spend their time.

If eating healthy is important to you, you'll make the time to slow down and be in the kitchen. You can do this with simple tools and simple food. I also believe that you can create systems, so it doesn't take a ridiculous amount of time either. For example, we cook sausage once a week. We crack five dozen eggs at a time.

The Junk Drawer

We all have one, at least one junk drawer that is a catch all for miscellaneous things that appear in our home.

- "I'll remember that's there."

- "I'll put that where it goes later."

- "I have no idea what this is, but I'll save it in case it's important."

- "This doesn't have a place, so I'll just stick it here."

We have a junk drawer in our kitchen and one in our office. I think it's perfectly fine to have a junk drawer as long as you clean it out on a regular basis. For me, that's about once every month or two. I take everything out, sort it, and relocate most of it.

Again, minimalism is about intentionality. I intentionally put things there when I don't have a lot of time to decide where it should go or to take it where it belongs. If it fits in a drawer, it's an okay trade off to me that I save time in that moment and I will address it later in the month.

Cookbooks and Recipes

I think most of us cling to these out of hope or sentimentality. It's a rare cook these days who relies on paper recipes and actually uses them! If you must, keep a small stash. Where you can, go digital. Don't let "what if I need this" and "I'll use this someday" contribute to clutter in your kitchen.

This is easy for me because I'm not very sentimental and I'm comfortable scanning things and keeping them in Google docs so I can access them anytime. If it's difficult for you, that's okay. Own that it's a sensitive topic, keep them for now, and move on to the rest of the house. We all have our areas that we're not quite ready to purge.

The Pantry

Dry food storage is something I've yet to master. I will go through a culling and clear out everything we don't need or use and then a few months later, cans and boxes seem to have weaseled their way in somehow. Whoever could be doing that?!?

I still buy things at the store thinking we'll eat them and letting them go untouched. I deal with this in one of two ways:

Donate it. If we can afford to get rid of food or if it's been there for more than six months, we donate it to St. Vincent de Paul. While it's painful to give away food, it feels better to give it to a family in need than to toss it in the trash. Of course, we only donate edible food that hasn't expired!

Meal plan with it. The other thing I do is to force myself to create a meal plan for the following week using as much as I can from the pantry. If I have a bag of red lentils, I'll figure out a way to use them. After all, I must have had something in mind when I bought them! Shop from your pantry first, then go to the store for anything else you need. You'll clear it out in no time!

Kitchen Specific Questions

What is this item used for?

How often do I use it?

Can I use something else to perform the same function?

Does this provide value to my life on a daily/weekly basis?

Am I keeping this out of obligation or expectation?

Am I saving this just in case?

Cleaning System

When it comes to feeling stressed out by your kitchen, it likely has more to do with dirty dishes and cluttered counters than what is in your cupboards and drawers. You can minimalize most of your tools and utensils but still leave your dinner dishes out and feel frazzled in the morning.

Minimalism and cleaning are not the same thing. Keeping your kitchen clean is certainly easier if you have less to clean but few of us are actually cleaning all the gadgets that we own.

First, you need to be honest about your cleanliness threshold. For me, I can have dirty dishes in the sink, and it doesn't bother me, but I really don't like it when there are things piled up on the counter. I like to see flat, clear spaces.

My husband, on the other hand, can't stand any dirty dishes to be around. It drives him nuts, especially if there's just one or two. He will ask me in a surprised and exasperated way why they weren't finished.

Know what's important to you and the rest of the household and create a system for making sure it gets done. There are plenty of ways to do this. Just Google "Kitchen cleaning schedule," "checklist," or "hacks." Remember, no amount of decluttering is going to create a kitchen that cleans itself!

Garage

Commence big groan! Most people know that their garage is a problem area. The majority of Americans park in their driveway because their garage is crammed full of stuff. Before you start feeling anxiety over tackling this part of your home, take a deep breath and remember, you don't need to do this overnight.

You can set the pace for any area of your home. If the garage is a gargantuan problem space, decide that you're going to spend a certain number of hours on it and be okay with not completing it at first. You may need two whole years to slowly deal with your garage. You may also choose to roll up your sleeves, rent a dumpster, hire some teenagers, and slam it out in a long weekend!

Because my husband and I both had grandmothers who were clinical hoarders, we don't keep that much stuff in our garage. And even though we're committed to this, we still let stuff build up and have to clear it out about once every three months. Having a clean and organized garage takes a great deal of initial effort and then a commitment to keeping it that way!

Whose Domain Is It?

If you live alone, this is simple; it's your domain. If you are married or have roommates, you need to discuss who is responsible for this space. Most of us share the garage space with someone else, like our spouse, but really one person does most of the work in the garage and subsequently most of the cluttering.

In our home, the garage is my husband's domain. He stores all his tools, hunting gear, camping gear, bikes, canoe, etc. there.

I have two totes in the garage for seasonal decorations. Since my husband uses the garage far more than I do, I leave the organization to him. If he has a question about the stuff I store there, we talk about it, but I don't have a strong opinion about how the garage is laid out.

If for someone reason the clutter affects me (i.e., there is so much stuff on the floor that I can't open our standing freezer to get the meat out) then we talk about it.

While husbands often claim the garage as their own, plenty of wives dominate the space by storing totes of clothes, decorations, and lots of kid stuff. Get together and decide who is going to manage the space. If you're going to do it together, make a plan. You don't want too many cooks in the kitchen or minimalists in the garage each tossing out the other person's stuff and causing frustration.

What is the purpose of this space?

While most of the other rooms in your home have an obvious purpose, a garage can be used for many different activities. Here are just some of the possibilities:

- Park your car(s)

- Personal gym

- Woodworking area

- Storage unit (totes, tools, excess house stuff)

- Store tools and lawn maintenance items

- A finished space (i.e., playroom, guest room, etc.)

Once you have determined the use of the space, it's time to get intentional about the things that live there.

Organization

Previously I talked about the difference between cleaning, organizing, decluttering, and embracing minimalism. When it comes to the garage, it's hard to have a peaceful space if you don't tackle organization in addition to minimization.

I would recommend going through two phases. First, touch everything with a minimalist mindset trying to decide what stays and what goes. Then give yourself a break, at least a week or two. Then go back again with an organization mindset.

Because many different categories of stuff tend to live in this space and because we want so desperately to keep it off the ground, you must do some research and get creative about how to store and label all the items in your garage. I'm not going to list those ideas here because you can simply Google or Pinterest "garage organization" or "garage storage" and find lots of wonderful ideas.

Don't put this off forever though. You need to keep your space tidy even after you've gotten rid of anything you don't want. Most websites I visited recommended having zones for like items or activities, taking advantage of vertical space, and had suggestions for how to go about managing these!

I will leave you with this one simple guide that I found on unclutter.com[xviii] for grouping like-items together so you can at least put things back in some order until you come up with a permanent organization plan.

Group Like Items

Figure out how much space your car(s) will take and then work with what's left by placing items in spaces based on their types and uses:

Frequently Used: Keep items that you use frequently, such as shopping bags and pet leashes within easy reach – perhaps on hooks by the door.

Items Used Together: Create zones for groups of things such as auto care, gardening, and sports equipment so that like items are stored together.

Bulkier Items: Use the two back corners of the garage to store bulkier items such as a lawn mower or snow thrower.

Rarely Used: Place rarely used items, such as holiday decorations or snow tires, on higher shelves of sturdy shelving units or consider installing a ceiling storage system. Just make sure your garage door doesn't interfere with the ceiling storage.

Tools and Bicycles: Tools such as shovels and rakes and bicycles are best stored by hanging on the wall.

Note: If you're using cardboard boxes as storage containers, you might want to seriously consider investing in some plastic bins that will keep insects and rodents from taking up residence in your house.

Garage Specific Questions

How long have those boxes been untouched?

Do I even know what's in there without looking?

Did I actually put up those decorations last year?

Are there tools I really don't use?

Could I get rid of tools and easily borrow them from a neighbor?

What are all these chemicals, cleaners, and paints for?

Am I still into this hobby?

Office (Room or Area)

No one likes working in a cluttered space. Yes, there are plenty of articles about how geniuses like Bill Gates and Albert Einstein work at messy desks, but in general, it's not the state most of us want our workspace to be in. Whether you have a whole room as an office or simply a computer/working area, it's important that this space is easy to use and provides a peaceful environment.

If your school room and your office are the same room, read this section first and then move on to the homeschooling chapter in section three.

I'm going to go out on a limb and assume that most of you have too many office supplies. Even if you work from home, it's likely you don't need drawers full of "productive nick knacks." We have different jobs, and therefore we need different tools to accomplish our job. The first thing you need to do is determine what type of work is going to happen at your office.

In my office, I write books and articles, record podcasts, edit family photos and photo books, do bookkeeping for our fence company, and surf the internet for pleasure. Though to be honest, most of my fun internet time is spent on my phone.

Consult Everyone Involved

If your office space is used by more than one person in your family, take the time to ask them what their needs and wants are. My husband and I like different brand pens. We keep some of both, but we get rid of any pen that's not one of those two brands.

Different family members will use the space for different things. Perhaps your son will want a place to put homework he is working on, or your husband wants a notepad to take notes on. Get everyone's feedback and try to incorporate it all into your minimalist plan for the office!

Get Rid of Drawers

Imagine your desk has no drawers (really just a table) and ask what stuff you would keep. This arrangement forces you to deal with the stuff on the desk, and it motivates you to avoid putting stuff there in the first place. Have a small container for pens and maybe one highlighter. What else do you need?

Okay, okay, some of us do need more than just a few pens. As I mentioned, I do my podcast at my desk, so I have a microphone. I store this on a shelf that's on the side of my desk. It's important to recognize the work you'll be doing here and to make sure you have the tools you need for that work and only the tools you need for that work.

Go Completely Paperless (or mostly)

We are working hard to become a paper free household, or at least in our office. My three girls like coloring every day, so I doubt we'll see an end to that type of paper. Now when I get mail or paper, it immediately falls into one of two categories: action required or scan.

I have a great app on my phone that easily scans documents and automatically puts them into Evernote for me. Once that is done, I toss the paper. And let me tell you, this was hard to adjust to! I was paranoid that... I don't know... the internet would break and I'd lose all these records.

I'll be honest; it was easier to go paperless for our business than for our personal papers. I don't know why it was harder for me to let go of filing personal bills, notes, and even major contracts. Why do I need to hold on to my gigantic house mortgage folder? They gave me an electronic copy. If it's backed up, I really really don't need that paper copy.

The more I scan and get rid of, the more I have come to like a paperless lifestyle. There is so much less to keep track of! There are so many fewer piles around the house. We have a folder for important papers we have to keep (i.e. birth certificates, social security cards, baptism records, etc.)

Downsize Your Supplies

Again, you probably don't need most of the office supplies you're keeping around. When was the last time you three-hole-punched something? Do you really need eight spare erasers? If we're aiming at becoming paperless, we probably don't need as many folders and three-ring binders.

Ditch The Desktop

Several websites I read suggested ditching the desktop computer in favor of a laptop. Some even went as far as to say you can work from anywhere in your home and you don't need an office at all! This seems extreme to me, and I know it won't work for all of you. I've had a desktop since fifth grade, and it's hard for me to imagine really letting it go for just a laptop. Perhaps this is old fashioned of me.

Here's a great example of a decision I am making based on

feelings, especially fear. When I examine my reasons for not wanting a laptop, they're all emotional and not based on fact at all. It's good to acknowledge when we're holding onto something for the wrong reasons even if we're not ready to make the switch yet.

I think I will consider a laptop strongly if my desktop dies but I'm not ready to make the switch proactively. I like the idea of it, and it would be more minimal, but I still need some convincing!

Cut The Cord

Where possible, go wireless. Not all of us have the money to do this right now but if you do, purchase wireless headphones and a wireless keyboard. If there's anything else with a wire, see if you can get a wireless version of it. This will free up space, clutter, and headaches in your minimalist office!

An Experiment

I love this suggestion from The Minimalists. "As an experiment, why not give this a shot: get rid of everything today (box it up or simply get it out of the way), then slowly reintroduce items to your workspace as needed over the next few days. Then get rid of anything you didn't reintroduce—anything you don't use this week."[xix]

I like these extreme ideas because they force me to slam straight into my emotion of fear. "But what if I need it later?" That isn't a good enough reason to keep something. If you didn't have one, it's likely you'd do without it entirely or come up with a creative solution for the few times you need it.

Office Specific Questions

Can I get cordless versions of any of these?

Do I really need a landline?

Can I get rid of machines by purchasing a scan/fax/print in one machine?

Could I digitize this and file it online?

Do I have multiples of this office supply and do I need them all?

Can I use a paperless version (Google drive, an app on your phone, paperless billing, etc.?)

Living Room

Hopefully, by now, you're getting into the swing of decluttering a room and turning it into a more minimalistic space because I'm going to be less specific about what to do with this space. When it comes to every living room I've been in; no two are the same. They all have different purposes, design styles, furniture layouts, etc. And many homes have both a living room and a family room. Even as I type that, I'm not sure what the difference really is!

As always, start by determining the purpose of the space. Who is going to spend time there? What do you want to encourage in this space? I wanted to encourage my kids to read books in our family room, so I made the bookshelves low and provided comfy chairs and pillows.

This space more than any other is going to benefit from a daily, if not twice daily, tidy up session. My kids tidy the living room (which we call the play room) before lunch and before dinner. In fact, they don't eat if it doesn't get tidied. I feel so much calmer and peaceful when this space isn't a disaster, so we prioritize it being tidy.

Living Room Specific Questions

Where do I want guests to sit? Will they have drinks in this space?

If this room ends up being a dumping ground for things like backpacks, where should those go instead?

Is it okay to play music in this space without bothering others?

Do I need some more shelves or baskets?

Where do blankets go?

Do I love the artwork on the walls?

Do I care how the bookcases are organized?

Where do I want all the gaming systems and games?

Can I utilize the space under the couch?

What is my firewood system?

Any Other Room or Storage Space

We've covered the most common areas found in American homes. There are certainly several rooms or spaces you may have that I haven't specifically addressed. Basements, attics, craft rooms, and storage sheds all come to mind.

By now you should have gotten the hang of what criteria to use for whether something stays or something goes. You can apply the generic Getting It Done worksheet to these spaces.

If you have any specific questions, always feel free to pop over to the Catholic Minimalism Facebook group at www.facebook.com/groups/catholicminimalism/ to ask a specific question. The group and I will dive right in and try to get you a helpful answer!

I hope these room guides will be helpful and I look forward to seeing your before and after photos! Now that we've talked about minimalizing our things, it's time to talk about minimalizing our digital files!

CHAPTER 15:
DIGITAL MINIMALIZATION

Now that we've talked about tackling the physical things we own let's move on to discussing all our digital stuff. Yes, we have accumulated quite a lot in the last years. Between our email, phone apps, pictures, and all the documents on our computer... not to mention the cloud... we are drowning in a digital sea of files!

Many nights I find myself spending more time browsing Netflix than I do watching anything. There are too many things to choose from! It's overwhelming, and in the end, I've robbed myself of true leisure and relaxation by wanting to find the best possible show I can.

I don't need to tell you that most of our email inboxes are a mess. We feel anxious just thinking of all the undone tasks that are lurking there. It's an inbox of guilt is what it is.

We've allowed our desires to be everything to everyone creep into our digital life. We want to keep everything even though it causes us stress to sift through it all, especially when needing something important in a timely manner and we can't find it.

Just as you've scheduled time to minimalize your physical stuff, you need to set aside time to minimalize your digital work too. Here are some suggestions:

Declutter Your Email

Go through every email you own and deal with each one. File it or reply. Then go to www.unroll.me and unsubscribe from the dozens of places you receive email updates from! This is an amazing and free service. Going forward, stay on top of your email. If you can answer anything quickly, do it right away. Don't let it linger in your inbox taunting you for days.

Declutter Your Computer

When is the last time you went through all the documents on your computer? Have you ever spent the time to setup folders for all this information? Now is a good time to go through everything, get rid of old documents and organize what's left. I have made a huge effort to keep as much as possible in Google Docs or Google Spreadsheets, so I don't have any files on my computer to deal with. Clear out old programs you don't use and icons on your desktop.

Declutter Your Photos

It's so easy to take digital pictures now that we have thousands of them. Instead of printing them and enjoying them, they stay trapped on our phones and on our computers. Google "digital photo management" and learn how you can better organize your photos. You'll appreciate being able to find the ones you truly love and hopefully this will inspire you to print some out and hang them up so you can enjoy them!

Declutter Your Social Media

I'm going to include all phone apps and online browsing in this section. Cut down your friends, cut down your apps, and cut down the websites you visit. You know you need to do this, and you know it will bring you more peace. Avoid the news if you can. Stop watching so much television. Stop looking at your phone all the time. Less is more when it comes to all screen time. Delete as many temptations as you can!

I could write a whole book about screen time and how Americans have become slaves to the digital world. For now, let's all just acknowledge that less is more. We should be spending more time outside, having in person conversations, reading books, and praying. This is one area where I think efficiency is appropriate! Organize your digital stuff, so you don't need to deal with it as often.

Sterling Jaquith

The Nitty Gritty: Problem Solving Real Life Challenges

CHAPTER 16:
SENTIMENTAL ITEMS

This category of things we own can be the most difficult to sift through. God created us to love deeply, to feel strongly, and to embrace this beautiful journey of life. The more we live our lives, the more wonderful memories we create – and those often come with trinkets as reminders. When we lose loved ones along the way, we also inherit their mementos which now have a double meaning. They become even more important to us.

As we consider purging the unnecessary from our homes, it feels impossible to tackle these sentimental items. We need them! But of course, this isn't really true.

As I write this section, hundreds of people have lost their homes to hurricane damage in Texas and Florida. These families grabbed their loved ones, their pets, and what they could carry knowing they would return to a house that had been destroyed by wind and water. And yet amidst this tragedy, there is great joy.

They are filled with joy to be alive and unharmed. They are safe, and they will rebuild. They have been forced to learn the lesson that we are not what we own and, in the end, everything we own will turn to dust.

I am not against holding on to sentimental items as a rule but rather, we must examine not only why we are keeping an item but also what costs us to do so. Below are some guidelines for helping determine which sentimental items you want to hang on to. Remember, no one is forcing you to get rid of these things. Take as much time as you need. If you have to leave this category until last, that's okay. But as you decide to be intentional about what you keep, you must also be intentional about these items and not simply say, "It's sentimental."

Sentimental Guidelines

Memories are not actually contained in physical items. Sometimes holding on to all these items keeps us living in the past. They keep us from being truly free. Here are some things to consider when it comes to what you keep for sentimental reasons.

Digitize What You Can

We're scared of forgetting, of letting go. This feeling can be minimized when we capture the item in a picture that we can return to over and over again. Scan photos, slides, important papers, etc. Snap a picture of items you want to remember or show to your children without having to hold on to it. Put your kids in your dad's favorite easy chair and take a picture, then donate the chair. Put one of your mom's favorite necklaces in your hand and take a picture. That picture will help you remember what it felt like to hold it and think of your mother. Do this if you know the necklace is not your style, and you're never going to wear it.

Write It Down

Along the same lines as taking a picture, writing down your memories is another wonderful way to preserve them. My husband's grandparents do this and send them to us in little spiral bound books. We adore these stories, and they take up very little space. Instead of keeping a trinket, write about it and the joy it brought you or the family member it belonged to.

Share With Someone In Need

It's easier to let go of things we're emotionally attached to if we know they're going to a good home. While you can't stand the idea of dropping something off at a thrift store, giving it to a single mom in need will warm your heart. You will feel like you're honoring your past this way by helping someone's future.

Consider The End

As I mentioned earlier, my husband and I both cleared out the homes of our hoarding grandparents. There was so much stuff that I'm certain sentimental items got tossed out with the trash. When you're keeping something, consider what's going to happen to that item when you pass away. Do you intend to leave this to your children? Do they even want it?

Here is an exercise I go through: I imagine living in a cute two-bedroom condo in my 70's, and I try to imagine if I want to keep this item through all the houses in between now and then. I close my eyes and picture how much joy this item might bring to me then. If I can't picture it, I don't keep it.

Maintenance

How much work does this item create for you as you store it? If you have so much stuff that you rent a storage unit, you can actually put a price to this. If you have to clean out or rummage through your garage often because it's crammed full of sentimental boxes, consider whether that pain is worthwhile.

The Little Things

It's easy to say, "Oh this is so small, it doesn't matter." This tends to bite us in two ways. First, lots of little things really add up and suddenly our house is bursting with little things. Second, the philosophy of minimalism is not about whether or not you have space for something but rather about being intentional about what you choose to keep.

I choose to keep all the letters and cards my husband has given me. They fit in one tiny box. I know that when I am older, I will pull these out and they will warm my heart. I do not choose to keep all the school work and art work my children do. If something is particularly cute, I take a picture of it but I know that if I kept every sweet drawing I received, I'd end up with totes of artwork. And while my kids would get a chuckle out of seeing those in twenty years, it is unlikely they will want to store those totes in their house in the future.

Choose Your Favorites

I have a beautiful jade statue of Mary that was my grandmother's. Not only is it beautiful statue in its own right but it reminds me of this sweet woman who prayed her rosary every night and sang like a nightingale. I will never get rid of it. Even if none of my children want this and it gets donated after I die, I will not regret holding onto it all the years in between.

Sitting here, I can't think of even ten items I feel this strongly about that will likely stay with me throughout my whole life. Choose the things that touch you deeply and only keep those.

"To sentimentalize something is to look only at the emotion in it and at the emotion, it stirs in us rather than at the reality of it, which we are always tempted not to look at because reality, truth, silence are all what we are not much good at and avoid when we can. To sentimentalize something is to savor rather than to suffer the sadness of it, is to sigh over the prettiness of it rather than to tremble at the beauty of it, which may make fearsome demands of us or pose fearsome threats." – Frederick Buechner[xx]

A great exercise recommended by Rosie Leizrowice in her article *The Psychology of Sentimental Items and How To Let Go Of Them* is to write a list of your sentimental items from memory. "If you cannot even remember you own something, the chances are that it matters less than you think."[xxi]

The love we have for one another and for the beauty of life's experience is rooted in God. He created this magnificent world and humankind so we could experience love and beauty so we could be drawn to Him. Ask yourself whether you are growing closer to Him through love and beauty by keeping sentimental items. In the end, that should be the guide we always use.

CHAPTER 17:
HOLIDAY AND LITURGICAL DECORATIONS

As I confessed in my holiday book *Be Merry*, I used to have a real problem in the decorations department. I blamed this largely on the Pottery Barn catalog and the well-placed decorations display at Costco, Target, and JoAnn Fabrics. I would find myself drooling over cute bunny Easter decorations, glittery pumpkins, snowy white owl ornaments and even hearts and shamrocks at the Dollar Tree.

These idyllic scenes would play out in my mind of warm dinner parties, sweet memories with my children, and a deeper appreciation for what we're celebrating because of the perfect setting.

At first, I gave in to this temptation albeit with used

decorations from garage sales and thrift stores or cheap ones from the Dollar Tree. I'd toss everything about, and instead of being magazine worthy, my house looked like a seven-year-old decorated it. I admit that interior design is not one of my natural skills.

This would actually cause me to have mom style tantrums telling my husband that our house looked stupid and feeling like a failure for not being able to create holiday magic. Guess what? God does not want you turning into a momzilla over decorations. It kind of misses the point of choosing joy.

The second thing that taught me to largely let go of seasonal decorations was having lots of babies! Guess how much I care about decorating for Valentine's Day when I'm throwing up in the first trimester? Not. At. All.

You start to learn what you can live without when you're in survival mode whether that's a new baby, a husband deployed, caring for an aging parent, etc. The more I realized I didn't need, or even miss, putting up certain decorations, the more I agreed to get rid of. This also greatly pleased my husband who gained more garage space!

Creating A Warm Environment

I like the idea of decorations. I also like the idea that the tone of our home changes throughout the year, especially related to the changing liturgical seasons. This is a natural desire, especially for women as I mentioned in my book *Be Merry*:

> The brilliance of the devil is that he always takes something good and twists it. Women were designed to be receivers. We receive people into our homes; we

receive children into our hearts. Even if you don't have any biological children, you were made to be a spiritual mother to someone. That is part of the essence of womanhood.

That is the reason you want your home to be warm and inviting. You want people to feel welcome and to have a comfortable time at your house.

This is a good and pure intention, but the devil twists it. He whispers in your ear that you're a failure if you don't have a beautiful house with Pottery Barn decorations. People aren't going to be happy if your silverware and your glasses don't match. People won't feel welcome if you don't serve gourmet food with lovely garnishes.

Creating beauty in your world is not a bad thing – but when you do it by sacrificing your peace, it's not okay. So this year, when you are thinking about decorating or planning a party and bringing people into your home, remember that Jesus made women to receive people. Give them love and show them the light of Christ. Ask for help, "Jesus, help me make this event about you and not about me."

Choose Flat Items

The more I refine my holiday and liturgical decoration collections; I find myself chucking large items in favor of things that are flat. A well placed felt owl on the coffee table for Fall, a simple paper heart garland on the fireplace, some white paper doves around for Pentecost, etc. These are often simple, cheap, and just as good at creating the mood I want.

When you're out and about thinking about adding a decoration to your collection, hold it in your hand. Consider where you're going to put it during the holiday. Then consider where you're going to store it. You'll find flat items pass the test far more often than adorable ceramic Easter bunnies!

Choose Natural Items

One way to embrace the changing seasons is to decorate with what's available that season. Display pumpkins before you carve them. Put out fruit and vegetables that are in season in a bowl. Buy fresh flowers or pick some from your yard. If you made a special craft for a feast day or a saint day, hang them up for the month. Put your gingerbread houses up on the fireplace for two weeks.[xxii] These are all things that will come down naturally and don't need to be stored.

Be Honest With Yourself

I could write this paragraph for every section in this book. Dig deep. Look in the mirror. Say it out loud. Why are you really keeping this? Do you really need it? A lot of the time, you know exactly which items bring true joy and beauty to your home and which ones simply belong to a fantasy you have about a life in your mind.

CHAPTER 18:
WHEN YOU STRUGGLE FINANCIALLY

One of the reasons I wanted to write this book was to address a huge hole in most minimalism books: what minimalism looks like among the poor. Let us not dive into a debate on what it means to be poor. Of course, there are many different levels of poverty, but this chapter is going to focus on anyone who lives paycheck-to-paycheck, struggles to pay even basic bills, or may not even be able to afford their basic needs.

This chapter will not attempt to solve the issue of not having enough money but rather discuss a battle strategy for how a person can tackle a minimalist lifestyle if they are strapped financially.

Many families who fall in this spectrum live high stress lives with little stability. These families don't have the luxury to toss extra kitchen tools knowing they could buy them again later... because they can't. These families can't go to The Container Store and spend $200 on bins and baskets to better organize their things. They can't buy nice clothes at Lands End that will hold up longer than cheap Walmart clothes even if they know the nice clothes are worth it.

These families need a slightly different approach to bring some simplicity and freedom to their homes. Here are some practical things they can do to find peace and freedom in the chaos of financial stress.

Get A Bible

The first thing these families must have is a Bible. If you can't afford one, find a church and ask for one. They will give you one, I promise. If they won't for whatever reason, email me, and I'll make sure you get one. You cannot manage the deeply stressful life of not having enough money if you don't have a Bible to cling to.

Anchor yourself to the Gospels and the Proverbs. Read them over and over again. You will find your true worth on these pages. You will find weapons to fight the fear you feel and the jealousy that sneaks into your heart. The world is going to scream at you that you're no good, that you don't count, and that you're failing somehow; but those are lies.

Jesus loves you right where you are. He knows the truth: you cannot take anything with you to Heaven, so all this worry over worldly items is for nothing.

I'm not trying to brush you off with platitudes. Being poor is hard. Using WIC checks or food stamps is humbling. Not being able to afford to go to the doctor is scary. Wearing old and tattered clothing can feel shameful. Not being able to provide for your children can suck the air out of your chest.

Reading your Bible will not make these feelings go away. What it can do is empower you to recognize those feelings and to not give in to them.

The more we internalize Biblical truths about divine love and the power of suffering, the easier it is to see blessings in the storm. These truths help us short-circuit anxiety, so we don't allow our fear to turn into frantic and bad actions.

You don't need to buy anything to embrace a minimalist lifestyle. You don't need new clothes that all match. You don't need bins to organize your stuff; you can use cardboard cereal boxes.

Minimalism is a state of mind. It's about being content with less and knowing that the things we own do not define who we are. Our true value comes from Jesus.

Be Safe

When we live in stressful situations, and this is often the case for families who can't afford basic needs, high levels of anxiety can cause chaos. We flit from one thing to another, never knowing where to start, desperate to turn off the pain and allowing fear to rule us. We often move too quickly and create more problems for ourselves because we weren't thinking clearly. Alternatively, we can allow our fear to paralyze us thus avoiding tasks that need to be done... leading to more stress and problems.

If this sounds like you, your focus should be on remaining calm and providing a safe environment for your family.

Learn how to take deep breaths. That may sound silly and unimportant, but if you are constantly breathing shallowly, you are flooding your system with cortisol. Basically, your body thinks you are running from a tiger constantly. We were not designed to live in perpetual fear; we need to learn to calm down. We need to calm our mind so our body does not jump to fight or flight mode.

As we work on remaining calm, we need to look around and assess our home and our lifestyle. Is my family safe?

Safety comes from managing your environment (i.e., your home, your car, etc.) and managing the people in your life (i.e., avoiding abusive friends and family members).

It does not matter what the condition of your kitchen or your wardrobe is if your family is not safe. If your kitchen is so messy that kids have access to knives or you cannot keep your dishes clean, it isn't safe. If you have so many piles on your floor that you could trip on them while holding your baby, then your floor has become unsafe.

When the budget is tight, and you are likely living in "survival mode" (just barely making it each day), your focus needs to be on staying calm and being safe. Once you can manage those two things, you can tackle some of the more detailed aspects of minimalism.

Organization Is Key

When you are broke, and you don't know when that will change, it's likely you won't feel comfortable purging a lot of your stuff. For you, organization is going to be key. Here are some tricks for taming your clutter.

- Use cardboard boxes to organize your stuff. It doesn't need to look pretty. We all get cardboard boxes whether we order something online or we buy cereal each week. Spend a little time on the internet to find out how you can turn boxes into storage. When you can't get rid of things you might need later, organization becomes key.

- You need to have a place for everything, and you need to tuck away as much as possible out of sight. Clutter causes stress and anxiety. We want to utilize spaces like under the bed, high up in a closet, or creating extra levels to your kitchen cupboards.

- Do get rid of things that are broken or that you genuinely don't use and won't use. Not having a lot of money isn't an excuse to hold onto cheap McDonald's toys or things that don't work. You don't get out of having to purge anything. Do go through your home and get rid of things that are broken and you can't fix them or things you genuinely won't use even in the future.

Embrace Humility

One of the greatest aspects of the Catholic Church is her commitment to serving the poor. We all know that this is a major tenant of our faith. Some of us may be better at actually doing this than others, but most of us know serving the poor is important. When asked, we would admit we'd like to be better about it.

Many families who struggle don't ask for help out of pride. They are ashamed of their situation, and they don't want to admit that they need help. And yet, if someone were to ask me for something simple like diapers, a meal, or some clothing for themselves or their kids, I would immediately try to help.

Do not be afraid to reach out to others. I recently saw a mom who posted on Facebook that she needed a size eleven church shoes for one of her boys. Another mom, whose family was financially stable, happened to have a pair her son had outgrown and happily offered them. It was a beautiful moment. There was no shame. There was no judgment. It was just two women helping each other out.

We have largely lost this sense of community. We don't communicate as openly as we used to; it's harder for us to help one another.

People want to be helpers. We see this so naturally in children, and yet when we become adults, we suddenly become afraid to ask for help. I admit I'm pretty bad about asking for help. My husband will often point out to me that I often choose to get no sleep and turn into a crazy lady instead of asking for help from friends or family and he's right! But this is a terrible way to live.

We have bought the lie that others are too busy to help and yet when anyone ever asks for my help, I am always happy to do it! I don't know why I rob others of the same opportunity to do a good deed.

I grew up in a small apartment with a single mother. We often had our electricity shut off and ran out of gas on the side of the road. Not having enough money is gut wrenching and scary. Families who have experienced this know that it is a luxury to pursue a magazine perfect minimalist home of expensive furniture and beautiful artwork. It is difficult to spark joy when you are worried about buying food.

I believe that no matter how little we own, we can still be intentional about what we keep in our homes and we can find peace in Jesus. He calls us to suffering and poverty sometimes. We must be brave enough to love Him anyway. We can still choose to find value in people and in our faith instead of wishing we owned more stuff, even basic things that would greatly improve our lives.

There is no true peace and no true freedom apart from Christ. When we have nothing but Him, we truly learn that there is nothing more we need.

CHAPTER 19:
WHEN YOU HAVE A HUGE HOUSE
WITH MORE SPACE THAN YOU NEED

I'm embarrassed to say this is my current situation. My house is 3,700 square feet – whoa! This is certainly not the type of home I prefer, and I miss the simplicity of our 1,600 square foot house in Oregon. But when my parents said they needed to live with us, I knew pretty quickly that I wanted a house with two kitchens. They eat very differently from my family, and I knew we would all live much more harmoniously if they had their own eating and cooking space.

Since this was my main criteria for our next house, as soon as we found one in Boise, we offered for it the day it went on the market despite its large size. Now my parents live in 1,100 square feet in the basement, but that still leaves a gigantic 2,600 on the main and upper floor. This is still much more square footage than I want or need.

How do you practice minimalism when you feel like you live in a mansion? Here's what I've come up with:

Empty Spaces

As soon as we moved in, I told my husband, "We are not going to buy or keep more stuff just because we have space to store it." We purposefully have chosen that many cupboards, shelves, and closets will have nothing in them. They are off limits!

Half-Filled Closets

We have four bedrooms and four closets, but we have only filled one of them. My own closet is full because we use it for clothes, liturgical items including seasonal books, presents I'm storing and toys that are out of rotation. My guest bedroom closet is barely 1/3 full. My girls' closet is half full. The last closet is in our school/art room, and while that was pretty full at the time I started writing this book, I have since pared it down to almost half full.

Barely Used Rooms

We have four bedrooms, a large living room, a small living room and a dining room that is also a pretty big living space. Another way we have decided not to grow into our space is to leave some rooms pretty bare. Our smaller living room is called our Sacred Room. It is for praying and reading. It is always a quiet space, and this rule is enforced with the children.

My three girls are in the same room. One bedroom is very bare and is used as a guest room. It has a bed and a barely filled dresser. We have a mini crib that our new baby sleeps in here as well, but as soon as he's a good sleeper, he'll be in the girls' room too!

The Sacred Room and the guest room are the two most peaceful rooms in the house because they are quiet and they have very little stuff in them. Even the art on the walls is very simple. I don't have to clean these rooms very often, so I also have positive feelings about these rooms.

Now if you have a large home and you truly do need and use all that space, read through the regular minimalism exercises to make sure you declutter and organize well to maximize the rooms you use.

I challenge you. If you own a large home but want to embrace minimalism, ask yourself these questions:

Do I need to use all my rooms?

Do I need to fill all my closets?

What cupboards in my kitchen can I keep empty?

If I needed to move to a smaller house, what would I get rid of?

I promise that owning less stuff is more peaceful. You have less clutter to clean and organize. You will feel calmer in your space. You don't need to fill all the spaces you have. Challenge yourself about why you own the things you own regardless of whether or not it's easy to store them.

CHAPTER 20:
FOR HOMESCHOOLING FAMILIES

I have never pretended to know what schooling choices I will make for my children. I have started my journey, however, choosing to homeschool. For those of you who choose this, you've likely already discovered that a vast amount of books, paper, art supplies, curricula, and teaching aids have intruded into your home.

This is especially true if you suffer from Curricula Commitment Phobia. Many of us start by collecting different curriculum options either because we are struggling with ones we've already purchased or we discover something that sounds better than what we have. Perhaps, we simply have the type of personality that always wants to try something different.

I have met a lot of homeschoolers, and very few seem to start out with one program and stick with it for 12+ years! In an attempt to provide the best and most tailored education for our kids, we end up with a lot of stuff!

Not only do we often feel guilty as we stare at our bookshelves of material, but we also feel weighed down by the sheer volume of it all. The clutter shouts at us all throughout the school day, and our ideal, peaceful, educational environment ends up looking more like a dusty antique shop with little room to move around.

This may not be a problem for all homeschoolers but choosing this lifestyle does present a unique challenge when it comes to pursuing a minimalist lifestyle. On the following page are some strategies for helping us embrace both minimalism and home education!

BE HONEST

The first step to tackling homeschool materials and spaces is to get real with yourself. I know I feel awful when I've purchased something in good faith, especially if I have had to sell my husband on the idea, only to realize that for whatever reason, it's not a good fit. It's difficult to admit that I was wrong and to give away or sell something for less money. But this gets at the heart of minimalism.

We cannot keep things for emotional reasons, especially out of fear.

We must think rationally about what we keep and be intentional about what lives on our bookshelves. Feelings will come and go; often, they lie about the reality of the situation.

Take a deep breath and be honest with yourself. Why are you keeping this?

While I don't think the Kon Mari method of touching each thing you own and asking if it sparks joy is a great way of determining what stays and goes, I do think we can turn to our feelings to help sort out some challenging areas. Our feelings can sometimes clue us into the deeper story of what's going on with our homeschool stuff.

As you go through your school materials, in addition to asking some of the questions I lay out later in this chapter, pay attention to what feelings bubble up when you look at something. The first question you have to ask yourself is, "Are these feelings based on reality?" You may feel something quite strongly, but it may be a warped version of the truth.

For example, you have some math manipulatives that make you feel very happy but perhaps this joy comes from the fact you used them in your childhood and not because you're using them with your own children. Do you want to keep it out of nostalgia? There's no wrong or right answer here, but you need to understand WHY you are keeping this item.

Perhaps you feel a knot in your stomach when you look at a particular reading curriculum. Maybe you're not using it. Perhaps your child is really struggling with it. You're not sure if you should keep it but you spent so much money on it that you feel like you have to stick it out. The feelings of guilt about getting rid of it or the frustration you feel about your child's lack of progress should not determine whether you keep this or not.

Remember, you must act like a scientist.

Is this working? If not, what are the chances it will work in the future? Perhaps you can't afford another curriculum. Could you sell this one? Could you cobble some exercises together for free on the internet? Be rational about your decision. Don't let your feelings make the choice for you.

VERSION CONTROL

It can be easy to want to save curriculum that you might use in the future even if it's not the program you're using now. I would encourage you to research what the current version of that curriculum is. Companies make money by updating curriculum every few years. New homeschoolers usually want the newest version. So it would be more prudent to sell your copy now and purchase a current but used version in the future if you want to use it again. If you hold on to your version, you yourself may not want to use in five years if the newest version seems stonger.

DUPLICATES

C'mon now friends, do you really need four different kinds of writing curricula? Perhaps you do because you have children with different learning styles but if you're simply holding on to it because you bought it and you don't want to admit defeat, it may be time to let it go.

OUT OF SIGHT

For my frugal friends out there, perhaps you have done a rock star job of managing many different types of curricula for your many children. You rotate them based on age and skill level like a boss! Your problem is that you even though you have chosen your stash thoughtfully, you can see all of it in your school space.

Oh, the clutter! This would drive most people batty!

Your focus needs to be on hiding materials you aren't using. Can you fill shallow boxes or bins and put curricula under a bed? Can you add a shelf very high up in some of your closets to store materials you won't be using this year?

I have a friend who actually installed kitchen cabinets in her school room so she could put everything in cupboards that could be closed to make the room feel tidier. I thought this was a brilliant way to make the space feel more peaceful and less busy.

Organization is key when it comes to large amounts of stuff that you really do want to keep. This is worth some Googling time. There are so many websites dedicated to organize your home, even articles specifically about homeschooling supplies.

COME CLEAN

I'm very blessed that my husband is supportive of our homeschooling adventure. He trusts me to make most of the decisions about what we study, but he asks me to be thoughtful about what I purchase. This is a fair request since I am often guilty of getting excited by something new and shiny, then purchasing it without giving it enough consideration. I'm much better about this than I used to be, but there is something so tempting about educational materials that, while I'm frugal in almost every other area of our finances, I can fall into a trap when it comes to buying school stuff.

Because my husband has asked me to be careful, when I do blow it, I feel awful. The guilt hangs on me like a fifty-pound chain around my neck. I want to hide it. I don't want to tell him. I don't want to admit that I was careless.

Sometimes I made the best decision possible with the information I had and later, I discovered new information that made my previous purchase a bad decision in hindsight. Whatever the reason, ending up with something I won't use makes me feel so yucky that I eventually start to feel yucky about the whole school room!

The solution is to come clean. I sit him down, and I calmly explain the situation. I accept responsibility if I was impulsive or I explain what changed that turned my wise decision at the time, into a bad purchase. When I do this without getting heated or defensive, he is always kind and understanding.

He may still be disappointed, as often I am myself, but I feel so much better having gotten it out in the open. I can move on and my school room doesn't have the same cloud of guilt over it.

Don't put this off. If you're feeling bad about something, resolve it. The guilt may be with yourself or with your spouse. Either way, deal with it, create a plan not to let it happen again if possible, and move on.

SUPPLY AND DEMAND

Let's get real. I can almost guarantee you have too many school supplies. I'm talking tape, pencils, markers, scissors, highlighters, rulers, hole punchers, folders, binders, stickers, etc.

I love this quote from minimalist homeschool blogger, Allie Cassazzah:

"Laura Ingalls, amazing American writer, had just one piece of chalk and a slate board which she shared with her sister to learn with. Abraham Lincoln read Aesop's Fables over and over again because it was the only book he had. He did math by writing out sums on a shovel with a piece of coal."

The world will tell you that more bells and whistles mean a better education but if you're losing your mind cleaning and managing all this stuff, is it really better? Children are drawn to pure and tools. Give them five markers and one pencil. You don't need to bring entire art section of Target home in hopes of keeping them busy or exposing them to art.

Expose them to things that are true, good, and beautiful through the simplicity of books. Give them a blank sheet of paper that inspires their imagination.

SIMPLE SCHEDULING

Minimalism is not just about stuff; it's also about the intentionality of time. We often talk about the things we own because we spend a great deal of time acquiring them and then taking care of them. But our time itself is also something we must be intentional about. If you are tackling too many subjects or trying to fit in too many activities within each subject, you might just start losing your mind.

How can you simplify what you're teaching?

We want to stick every subject under the sun into our plans because we want our children to be well rounded and we don't want holes in their education. The truth is, there are holes in every single education. A person cannot, and will never, have a depth of knowledge about all subjects. Your job is rather to teach them to love learning so they can continue education themselves for their entire lives.

I use the Motivation Equation to help me decide what things are important each year for my children to learn. In Chapter 26, you can read about how to use this equation to determine your motivation (or lack thereof) for subjects and activities in your homeschool journey including extracurricular.

Remember that if you are homeschooling your children, you're providing them with so much more education than simply what's found on your bookshelves. Trust in that. The rhythm of your very lifestyle is an education for them. Don't feel as if you need to lean on more stuff, even books, to give them a deep and meaningful experience.

CHAPTER 21:
FOR LARGE FAMILIES

I want to start off by saying thank you for choosing to have a large family. Though I do not believe, in any way, that families need to be large in order to be holy, you have chosen a difficult path and the world does not reward you nearly enough for your sacrifice. So I thank you for your time, effort, and love in raising many children for the kingdom of God. May the Lord bless your family!

When I discovered minimalism, I was so excited that I started to read many books and blogs on the subject. Very quickly I discovered that most recommendations seemed to accommodate single people, couples with no kids, or couples with one or two kids. There didn't seem to be a lot of discussion around large families who simply did need a lot more stuff, especially if they were frugal in trying to pass things down from child to child.

I wanted to address this head on because I believe that even large families can embrace a minimalistic lifestyle and in doing so, find more peace in their homes.

I love this list of the benefits large families can have by living a minimalistic lifestyle that Rachel Jones lays out on her blog nourishingminimalism.com. With her permission, I've copied the whole list below because I really couldn't have said it better myself.

Less mess: Lots of 'littles' means lots of messes. The fewer possessions you have, the fewer things to clean and put away on a regular basis. Think about it. How many more minutes of your life do you want to spend picking up, or stepping on, the toys that have been dumped out of giant bins for the third time today?

Fewer broken items: Kids break things. It's inevitable. The more kids you have, the more broken things you're going to have. It's an extra stress that's just not needed.

Less fighting between siblings: I'm not going to

say no fighting between siblings, but when you reduce the number of things, especially toys, children become calmer. You'll hear less of 'That's mine!' and more pretend imaginative play. With less stuff to manage, it's also easier to keep each child's 'special' things put away in special places when they're done.

Fewer tantrums when you're out shopping: Children become used to not getting something every time you go to the store because it's part of the minimalist lifestyle. It's easier to say no to the little wants because it's part of the big picture.

Less laundry: When there's too much clothing, that's when the laundry pile becomes out of control. Too many choices lead to clean clothes mixed in the dirty clothes, the laundry pile doubles, and there's too much to fold and put away. Reducing the amount of clothing makes laundry so much more manageable.

Less to do: Less cleaning, less running, less organizing, less searching for missing things, less maintenance. Just less to do overall.

Less grumpiness: Let's face it; cleaning up all those messes, finding broken things, breaking up fights, surviving tantrums, running all over town. Those things all make us grumpy, tired moms. With fewer of those struggles, we are much happier moms. Happier moms equal happier kids!

More quality time: When you have a lot of children, maximizing your time with each one is incredibly important. By letting go of the tasks that aren't of value, you end up with more time to really connect with each of your children.

More help: When children aren't overwhelmed by too much stuff, it's much easier for them to jump in and help. You'd be surprised what chores the littlest of kids can manage when it's one simple step, not layers of clutter to pick up and then cleaning.

More space: It's pretty much guaranteed in a large family that children will be sharing spaces. Less stuff means more space, and every little bit of space counts when you have a large family.

More money: As a minimalist, you will begin to make quality purchases over quantity. As a result, you will take better care of those things. You won't find yourself buying just because something is on sale; you will buy out of need. You won't replace items because you can't find what you need. All of this adds much-needed room to the budget.

More effective systems: Organization to every area of life becomes a necessity for survival the more children you have! Flying by the seat of your pants just doesn't work anymore. Trying to organize when you have too much stuff is pointless and becomes a mess in no time at all. But once you pare down to the right number of items, organization becomes so much easier, and routines become manageable.

More joy and peace: As things start running more

smoothly, the budget gets a little bigger, and the kids are calmer, there's room for more joy and peace in the home.

Those benefits sound lovely! I want those things for my own household. Let's dive into the practical strategies that will help your family live life more fully with less and manage what you do own with finesse!

CLOTHING MANAGEMENT

Make sure you read the Clothing section of this book in the beginning of Chapter 14 to get a general sense of creating a minimalist wardrobe. Those principles are relevant to everyone in the family. For large families, even after embracing a "less is more" policy on clothes, you still need a good storage system for managing both sizes in use and future hand-me-downs.

When it comes to saving clothes, especially for two genders, those plastic totes really start to add up! One question I ask myself earnestly is whether or not something will be out of style in 2-4 years when I have another baby of that gender or when one of my daughters reaches X age to wear these clothes. I have begun to battle this preemptively by buying simple and classic clothes.

When I find pieces that I won't sew to fix up, won't be in style, or rarely got worn, I donate or sell them. I can't afford to throw away everything and buy it again for every child, but there are some pieces I let go of knowing I'll buy something else at a thrift store down the line for extremely cheap.

And really that's the ultimate question I ask myself. Is the pain of keeping this worth the price I'd have to pay in the future if I have to rebuy it? These last two years we have been extremely tight on money so often the answer is to keep the item, especially if I'm not low on space.

I've still found myself donating (or selling) baby clothes knowing I can buy them for less than $1 if we have another baby, especially if it's a gender specific outfit. Who knows if we'll have three more girls before we have another boy.

TOY LAND

I already covered some ideas about toy management in Chapter 14, so I just wanted to add a few extra strategies for large families. First, the more kids you have, the less, the younger kids need. I remember when I only had one kiddo and toys bought me time. I needed that time to step away and cook or just breathe.

By the time we had four kids, the younger two just followed the older two around. They didn't need little kid toys. They just played with the big kid toys. Don't worry about short changing your little ones. They're getting a wonderful childhood filled with older siblings – what a gift! Toss those plastic toddler toys. They'll probably be happy with one stuffed animal!

Next, you need to <u>double down</u> on the other strategies I've mentioned in this book:

- Opt for experiences instead of presents

- Give your children a specific amount of space, and if they want something new, something else has to go

- Get creative about organization and use spaces

thoughtfully (the top level of closets, under the bed, add extra bookshelves everywhere, etc.)

- Fewer keepsakes because you really just can't keep boxes of stuff for each child

Buckets and buckets of clothing are often one of the biggest challenges for large families. This problem starts off innocently enough. You receive tons of clothes for your first baby. You begin shopping at sales and thrift stores with more children. When clothes are only $1, why not? Suddenly each child has 40 pieces of clothes, many of which don't even go together!

This really began to be a problem for us when we had three girls. I was trying to be intentional about taking care of clothes so they would make it through all three but somehow, the clothing piles kept getting bigger and bigger. Suddenly each girl had something like 14 pairs of pants and nine pairs of shoes!

I immediately laid out every single piece of clothing they each had on my bed. I noticed that there were many oddball pieces that, while they may be super cute, didn't go with a lot of the other pieces. Eventually, I came to realize that my girls preferred things that were pink, purple, and teal.

I realize you may not be able to pull this off for older children who want to pick out their own clothes, but I got rid of anything that didn't fit this color scheme. Now all their clothes are interchangeable.

CHAPTER 22:
LIVING IN A SMALL SPACE

For those of you who live in small spaces (i.e. a yurt, a trailer, a tiny apartment, etc.) you know that there are some principles of minimalism that come naturally to you because of your confined space. However, simply limiting space isn't the same thing as choosing what fills your space intentionally. If we are going to be intentional about what we keep and where we spend our time, we must go through the same steps as someone who lives in a large home.

The good news is that living in small spaces has become trendy, so there are many websites dedicated to showing you how to get the most out of your tiny home.

On the following page, I will explain two things you must do to find peace in your small space.

BE INTENTIONAL

Again, you need to go through your entire space and decide if the things you have should really be in your home. You don't get a cop out simply because you are already living in a small space that limits how much you own. You must still go through the process of deciding if each item in your home should be part of your life.

Do you use it? Is it broken? Do you have more than one? How many moves are you willing to take this through? How much does clutter bother you?

These are all personal questions, so there are no right or wrong answers. If displaying your Star Wars action figure collection in the living room makes you feel proud and brings you joy when you see it every day, rock on. If four pieces of mail on your kitchen country drive you bonkers, no problem. Acknowledge that and get a mail caddy.

BECOME AN ORGANIZATION MASTER

Your job is to become an expert at organization and storage.

You must train like a ninja! No item shall sneak past you. Everything will have a place, and everything will be in its place.

You must be creative to use all your space well. Ikea is a wonderful place to go for ideas even if you can't afford their furniture or storage solutions. Craigslist is a great place to get things for cheap. And never underestimate the different ways you can use cardboard boxes or items from the dollar store to get organized!

We live in a time when we have easy access to life hacks and great ideas through Pinterest and YouTube. Carve out some time to learn about these helpful tips, so you can create a space, no matter how small, that makes you feel cozy and peaceful. After all, every home should be a safe haven from clutter.

CHAPTER 23:
WHEN PEOPLE LIVE IN YOUR HOME PART TIME
(i.e. step children, exchange students, summer only, etc.)

While I was doing research for this book, I asked people what unusual living situations they'd like me to cover. I had several requests for how to work with part-time residents. That includes step children who are there every other weekend, college students who are home for the summer, and exchange students for however long they stay. It does pose an interesting challenge to consider and arrange a home around a part-time resident.

After asking around and doing some research, here are the strategies I found that you can employ to manage your unique situation! On the following page, I layout my suggestions based on how frequent a person is planning on living in your home.

CONSIDER THE TIME

The first thing to think about is how long is this person going to call this space home?

Short-Term

If it's a short period of time, a two-week visit perhaps, you may not need to rearrange a bedroom/bathroom/closet for this person. You could create some simple and temporary spaces knowing that this situation won't last long.

I was once living with a friend for two months while I was going to dog training school in San Francisco. It felt more like living in a hotel than living in a home, and that was fine with me. I knew it was a short-term situation and I didn't expect any of the spaces in the house to feel like my own. If this is the situation, you might make a few drawers and some closet space available. Your guest should pick up after themselves and not really disrupt the overall minimalist feeling of your home. Alternatively, even if they do… maybe you have a particularly messy teenager in residence, it won't last long, and I don't think it's worth anything drastic to accommodate a short-term situation.

Long-Term

If instead, the person will be staying for an entire year, it is likely worth the effort to make that person feel more at home. By providing them space for all their things so they can easily put everything away, you will enable them to keep their own space tidy and peaceful.

It's worth taking the time to lay out your expectations. Don't just tell this person why you want the home to be clean but rather explain your mission to live intentionally with less. Share your minimalist views with them. It can be a great educational opportunity!

You certainly can't expect them to get rid of their stuff and it's likely they don't have much anyway, but you can encourage them to find a place for everything and keep everything in its place. Hopefully, this will smooth their transition into the home and give you more peace as well.

On And Off

For those of you who have people who come and go in your home, you may favor the strategies above of the short-term resident or the long-term resident. What I want to add for this type of living situation is that communication is crucial.

You must communicate clearly to the person who is coming and going. If for example, you have a stepchild who lives with you every other weekend, you need to sit them down and discuss your expectations. I would encourage you to involve them in the decision-making process, so you know what's important to them.

Also consider, not just how you want your home and their particular space to feel but also their own personal feelings as well. Do you want them to feel welcome in your home? If you keep a very sterile looking guest room or workout room that they simply get to sleep in when they're visiting, are they going to feel like they're part of the family?

If they only come once every month, does it make sense to let them put up their favorite band posters and decorate their room to their own taste? There are no right or wrong answers here but remember, minimalism is about living intentionally and for me personally, that almost always means putting the people I love before my desire for stuff and comfort.

It would be naive to assume that everyone has a traditional family. Many of us come from divorced parents, have blended families, non-traditional jobs, or unique living situations. Don't let societal norms dictate how you live. Ask yourself what do you and the people you love value? Choose systems for your home that make sense for your lifestyle. And once you've created a system, be honest with yourself later about whether or not it's working. If people are feeling frustrated, adjust the system. You get to create the tone and the atmosphere of your home. Be intentional.

CHAPTER 24
WHEN PEOPLE LIVE IN YOUR HOME FULL TIME

Sharing a living space with anyone, including your immediate family, is difficult. Mixing personalities, living styles, and cleaning expectations can be tricky waters to navigate. This is true whenever you share a living space with someone else. For those of you who share your living space with other adults, either your family, or roommates, communication is vital.

Before getting together to discuss topics like house cleaning and how much "stuff" is everyone allowed to have, you need to first ask yourself, "Who has the power?"

If you are living in your parent's basement to save money to buy a house, your parents have the power. There isn't much you can do here to make major changes except ask politely and do a good job of stating your case. If their piles and piles of stuff are creating a dangerous situation for your children, perhaps you can approach the topic gently, with concern, and then offer to help them clean out that area.

If you are living with a roommate and you split the rent 50/50, then you equally share the power. Though power is never truly equal. One of you will have a stronger personality. One of you will have a stronger desire for cleanliness and order. One of you will be more desperate to stay in that apartment or house while the other may have an easier time moving out and finding another place.

Understanding the true situation of power will help manage your expectations for the outcome of discussing these issues. If you are the one with the power, use it wisely. Be kind, generous, and polite. Also, recognize that to live harmoniously, it's rarely a good idea to threaten and strong-arm someone into doing what you want.

Now if a situation is really dangerous or unlivable, setting clear expectations and consequences is necessary. If you are stuck in a particularly difficult situation, I recommend reading *God Help Me! These People are Driving Me Nuts!: Making Peace with Difficult People* by Gregory Popcak.[xxiii]

Once you have determined who has the power, ask yourself what you want. I highly recommend writing it down. This will help give you clarity before calling a meeting of housemates. Once you know your desired outcome, call a meeting. If you're not sure what this should look like, Google "Roommate communication" for lots of ideas!

Remember, you cannot force someone to suddenly value minimalism. It's a lifestyle choice. You also cannot force someone to believe in or practice Catholicism. Your job is to make your desires known and then to be gracious to the person you're interacting with.

CHAPTER 25:
PRODUCTIVE PROCRASTINATION

In college, my room was never so clean as it was during finals week. I still have the tendency to be very productive in non-essential areas of my life whenever I should instead be focused on something more important. I'm really good at reorganizing my bills and our finances when I should be focusing on cooking healthy food. I have often been found sorting every single piece of clothing in our entire household when I should be making progress on our homeschooling curriculum.

It's easy to give in to productive procrastination when we're avoiding minimalism. We may be avoiding it out of just plain not wanting to do it. Alternatively, we may be avoiding it because we know the next room on our list is going to be especially emotional or difficult to sort through.

Signs of Productive Procrastination

One clear sign that you're suffering from productive procrastination is if you keep finding things that need to be done outside of the room you're supposed to be working on. Perhaps you get it in your head that you need to do laundry and clean the kitchen instead of heading out to the garage. Maybe you start paying bills or making important phone calls instead of tackling your craft area. If you can't seem to even set foot in the room you need to work on, it's likely you have an emotional barrier that's causing you to procrastinate.

The second way we experience productive procrastination is when we are overly preoccupied with the stuff IN the room we're working on. It often occurs in one of these ways:

- We find ourselves cleaning instead of sorting

- We waste twenty minutes flipping through sentimental items

- We get overly focused on organizing instead of quickly putting things in an "organize later" pile

- You're constantly checking your phone for text or social media updates

We are not being responsible when we choose comfortable work as a way of avoiding the hard or uncomfortable things we're responsible for. One way you'll recognize productive procrastination is the uneasy feeling you'll have. You know when you're working on the wrong thing and letting a more important task go unfinished. Finishing won't give the same sense of "job well done" because you know, deep down, that you're doing it for the wrong reason.

Ways to Overcome Productive Procrastination

- Reread a chapter or two from the beginning of this book to remember why minimalism is important.

- Look up Proverbs 12:11 and especially Proverbs 14:23 for a kick in the bottom from the Lord.

- Take a run around the block or do ten burpees. I'm not kidding. Sometimes I need something physical to snap me out of my bad choices.

- Set a special reward for blitzing through the room (i.e. pizza, a bubble bath, buying fresh flowers, etc.)

- Turn off your phone

Sometimes we have hard and uncomfortable things we just need to do. Say a prayer to St. Maximillian Kolbe and ask for the strength to do the hard work for Jesus. Offer up your suffering to Mary. Then get to work. You're an adult, and you can handle this!

CHAPTER 26
THE MOTIVATION EQUATION

I talk about The Motivation Equation in my book Catholic Mom Challenge and often on my podcast Coffee & Pearls. It's an extremely effective tool for figuring out why you're not getting something done. I'll share the equation and then I'll break down its four components.

This is something discovered through Brian Johnson who encountered it while studying the work of Piers Steel[xxiv], a leading psychologist in procrastination and motivation. On the following page is the motivation equation:

$$Motivation = \frac{Expectancy \; x \; Value}{Impulsiveness \; x \; Delay}$$

Let's start by breaking down what's in the numerator: how much you believe you can achieve this goal multiplied by how much you value this goal. I like to look at value first.

Value

Is the thing I'm trying to accomplish truly important to me? I like to use the examples of teaching our children Latin and making sure they make their First Holy Communion.

Sure, most homeschool families think, "Wouldn't it be lovely if the children learned Latin?" It sounds romantic and we can justify how this will help them in their future. And yet when the years get busy and push comes to shove… we start to question, "How important is learning Latin anyway?" The vast majority of us don't know Latin, and we're doing just fine in our adulthood. We don't actually value this a great deal.

Alternatively, there is almost nothing that could keep us from leading our children to communion. We would put up with a grumpy and disorganized religious education leader. We would drag our children to evening classes despite their cranky attitudes. We would make them use a bad textbook to learn their faith if that's what our parish required. Sacraments are non-negotiable.

If you're struggling to get something done, either minimalism as a whole or a particular area in your home, ask yourself, "On a scale of Latin to First Holy Communion, how much do I value this?" It helps to see all the ways in which having too much stuff and being too busy is causing you stress. Imagine your life without that stress. How much do you value that life?

Expectancy

Do I genuinely believe it's possible to achieve this goal? This can be a hard one to really ask yourself. Often I have to admit that, no, I really don't think I can achieve this goal. I don't believe I can lose thirty pounds and keep it off. I don't think I'll ever have a fantastic sex life with kids around. I don't believe I'll ever be able to carve out time for self-care and rest.

When you don't actually believe your goal is possible, you have to do one of two things: either get rid of the goal entirely, or break your goal into more manageable, and therefore believable, parts.

If you're just starting out and the idea of minimalism is new, it can be overwhelming. You might feel that to embrace this lifestyle you're going to have to get rid of everything and live in a 500 square foot tiny house in the woods. Sometimes I think this would be easier than trying to manage minimalism in my 2,000 square foot suburban home while still living real life with four kids!

The truth is, minimalism takes time. It's a skill and like any skill, we have to work hard to acquire it. Since you're reading this book, let's assume the goal of living a minimalist lifestyle is important to you. That leaves us with figuring out how to break down that goal into baby steps, so it feels more manageable. This mostly comes down to timeline and areas of your home.

If you feel like you can't do this, simply throw out a grand plan for now and just pick one area of your home to work on.

Pick an easy and non-emotional one like your junk drawer or all the socks in your house. These things are good to start with because they go quickly and they feel great!

As you're building up more self-confidence and excitement, choose a larger area to work on. When you experience a big win, now may be the time to consider a plan and pin down a timeline. The timeline can be extremely slow paced. You can do one room every month. That doesn't sound so bad right?

You need to expect that you're going to have success. Do what you need to in order to believe that this is absolutely a project you're going to finish.

Don't feel discouraged! God does not want you to live your life immersed in anxiety, guilt, frustration, or anger. The key to avoiding these things is to really understand and master yourself. Start by examining your motivation, or lack thereof.

Next, we'll look at the bottom of the Motivation Equation: Impulsiveness times Delay.

Impulsiveness

How distracted are you while trying to reach your goal? I talked about this a little in the productive procrastination chapter. If you're allowing yourself to be easily distracted, your impulsiveness is too high. If you are more into dancing around the room listening to Frank Sinatra than tackling your pile of jewelry and accessories, your overall motivation is low.

Oftentimes the things we allow ourselves to be distracted by are not bad, they're just not the best thing to be focusing on at the moment. If you find that minimalizing your home is just not happening and you've established that you believe you can do this and it's important to you, impulsively giving into distractions is the next biggest suspect.

If people are getting in your way, communicate to them that you can't be interrupted. If those people are three to five years old, they may need a movie to watch or to go to grandma's house while you get this room done. If it's your phone, turn off all notifications. Trust me; the world will survive without you. If you are your own distraction, give yourself a pep talk. Some of you will need soft love, and some of you will need tough love. Give yourself what you need.

You have to ask yourself who you want to be and what you want to get done. Are you setting yourself up for success?

Delay

This is how long it will take you to reach your goal. If you have a huge house or if you've stuffed your small home to the max, you may think it's going to take years to go through it all. Depending on your available free time, you might be right! But if the amount of time you believe it will take to accomplish your goal is very long, your motivation to get it done will be small.

Just like believability, this part of the equation is improved by breaking down your goal into smaller pieces. Don't consider the whole house. Don't even worry about your whole closet. Set out to tackle shoes in one hour. That's all you need to do this weekend. That feels manageable right?

Now you don't have to wait years to feel a sense of a job well done. You can get that feeling in one hour.

Understanding the Motivation Equation can help you examine your lack of progress. If you're lacking the motivation to minimalize your home, check in with these four parameters and see which one needs tweaking.

In the many times, I've gone through this process, I've made the least amount of progress in the kitchen. Based on this equation I believe it's because I don't value it that much. We have a big kitchen, so I really can just keep everything. My expectancy is low. I don't really believe I'll have the guts to get rid of half of it. It has previously been easy to be distracted while working on one section and then I throw my hands up and leave the project altogether. These are areas I need to work on, but at least I'm not frustrated because I don't KNOW why I'm not getting it done. Rather, I know why and I just have to ask myself how much I want to change those barriers.

When something is important to you, you'll move mountains to get it done! Trust me, with Jesus on your side, you can do anything!

CHAPTER 27:
MINIMALIZING YOUR MIND

In our modern culture, we are racing from one thing to the next. Smart phones and the internet have trained us to consume large amounts of information. Our brains have been conditioned to be "on" all the time – chewing on thoughts and ideas. We rarely encounter silence and, when we do, it often makes us uncomfortable.

In *The Happiness Paradox*, Matthew Kelly says, "When you take a few moments each day to step into the classroom of silence and reconnect with yourself and with your God, what happens? The gentle voice within grows stronger, and you develop a deeper sense of peace, purpose, and direction. You're healthier, you're happier, and you have a richer experience of life. Physically, emotionally, intellectually, and spiritually, we know the things that infuse our lives with passion and enthusiasm. We know the things that make us happy. We just don't do them."[xxv]

We need to get control over our thought life. I'm convinced that if we can push out negative and toxic thoughts, we can more clearly see the plan God has for our lives. One of the main reasons I wrote this book is because, when I stepped back and asked myself why more people weren't striving for sainthood, I saw that most of us have so much stuff in front of our faces so many appointments on our calendar and so much noise in our ears that we don't even have any energy left to consider the lofty idea of sainthood.

Materialism and consumerism starts in our mind. It is our feelings of fear and inadequacy that drive us to buy more. We must set out to retrain our minds and to take each thought captive to Christ. We need to spend time pondering the good, true, and beautiful so that we don't need to worry about keeping up with the Joneses.

Scripture Saturation

When I first embraced Christianity, I was attending an evangelical Protestant church. I signed up for a weight loss challenge with several other women. We went through a twelve-week program designed to help us free ourselves from emotional eating. One of the first things the program encourages you to do is to memorize a scripture verse each week. The first verse I memorized was, "For the word of God is living and active, sharper than any two-edged sword, piercing to the division of soul and of spirit, of joints and of marrow, and discerning the thoughts and intentions of the heart." Hebrews 4:12

It was a long verse! In order to memorize the weekly verse, it was recommended that we repeat the verse 100 times per day. I had a small piece of paper that I had ripped ten tabs at the bottom. I would fold over each strip after saying the verse ten times. After all the tabs were folded, I had finished my memorization for the day!

Let me tell you, when you say a verse 100 times per day, two things happen: First, you memorize that verse really well. Second, you quickly come to understand that if you fill up your mind with the words of the Lord, that there isn't room for toxic self-talk. You can't ponder the hopelessness you feel, the fear you have, or the guilt you experience over not doing your best.

God did not design our bodies to withstand large amounts of sadness or anger. When we experience too much of those emotions, we actually start changing the physical makeup of our bodies. We flood our system with cortisol, we see big drops in dopamine being released, our sleep is affected, and eventually our appetite too!

Did God mess up when He created us? Of course not! He created us to live in the Garden of Eden. It is the result of original sin that we experience all these negative side effects. And while we can never escape sin, it is something we will struggle with our entire lives. It helps if we work to minimize the sins we commit.

One of the best ways to accomplish this is to saturate our minds with the scripture of the Bible. "Do not be conformed to this world, but be transformed by the renewal of your mind, that by testing you may discern what is the will of God, what is good and acceptable and perfect." Romans 12:2

Calendar Purge

It is very difficult to decrease the stress in your life and the chaos of a worried mind if your calendar is overbooked. If you are constantly running from one appointment to the next, from soccer practice to piano lessons, from working late to volunteering, you won't give your mind the chance to be calm and peaceful.

While most of our commitments are not bad individually, when we add up all the things we've agreed to, we see that there isn't enough room left in the week to both "waste" time with the ones we love and to "waste" time with God.

Yes, we must waste time with those who are important to us. Give them the open space to just be with us. Show them they are important by prioritizing quality time even if all you do is sit around and talk or play a board game.

Start saying "no." You don't even need to explain yourself. You don't need to make excuses. You are responsible for being a good steward of your family, and if you're too busy to fit them in, you're not doing your job. Take each commitment and run it through the Motivation Equation. Ask yourself if this is truly important. Consider the lives your children will lead as adults and consider your own path to Heaven.

American culture will not only tell you that you need to own thousands of things, but it will also tell you that you need to participate in dozens of activities to be a "good citizen." Your kids need sports, music, art, foreign language, and mountains of homework from a good school to be successful adults. You know this isn't true.

Be the gatekeeper for your family. Protect them from the idol of success and accomplishment. Show them how to put people before achievements.

Humans are incredibly intelligent creatures. Our minds are extremely powerful and yet we spend little time learning how to control our thoughts. We can find deep peace and freedom from learning how to focus on what's good, true, and beautiful. These are the things of God. You may spend a lifetime learning to master your mind, but it would be well worth your effort.

It will be difficult to truly embrace the minimalist lifestyle if you are still a prisoner of negative thinking. It will also be difficult to work on your thought life if you are too busy to read about or practice how to rewire your brain to be more positive and anchored in Christ. Ask yourself, what is getting in the way of you experiencing more peace and freedom through Catholicism and minimalism?

CHAPTER 28
LIVING FORWARD

After you've gone through all of your things, you might be wondering "what now?" The truth is that minimalism is a lifestyle; it never ends. It's a constant state of mind. It's about living intentionally.

Catholic minimalism is about living intentionally for Christ. Often the decision to keep or toss things might look unimportant, but it's fundamental to our desire to choose God over the world. It's about choosing love. The less we own, the more we can love. This is so counter-cultural that we don't want to believe this is true and yet it is. When we have less stuff to care for, we will have more time to care for people.

The secret to maintaining a minimalist lifestyle lies in systems.

This is different than efficiency. We are not creating systems so that we can cram more appointments in or have more stuff fit into our closet. We create systems in our homes, our calendars, and our phones that help us take care of the things we have chosen to keep and to be strict about what gets added to our home and our schedules.

Your job from now on is to be a scientist. You need to step back and be able to assess your life without letting emotions get in the way. Make objective observations. What is working? What is not working? Create and adjust your systems to continue your minimalist lifestyle. Need help? You can always pop into the Catholic Minimalist Facebook group and ask the group for help! Just visit www.facebook.com/groups/catholicminimalism/.

CHAPTER 29
CONCLUSION
BE NOT OF THIS WORLD

The world is full of shiny things. The more you live in the world, the more you think about and desire these shiny things. They become magnetic. You will start to cling to them strongly and become a magnet yourself. As you begin your minimalism journey, it will take great effort to pull yourself away from those things that you are you so firmly stuck to.

The only way we can truly find freedom from materialism is to follow Christ. The more we follow Him, the more we become like the wood of the cross. We are less like magnets, and so we can more easily walk through the world and not feel pulled by the shiny things. No amount of effort from the world can make metal stick to wood. Be like the cross, and you will feel free.

Christ is the only way we will find true peace and true freedom. We desire this deep down in our bones and in our very soul. It's why we are never satisfied no matter how many things we own. Matthew Kelly says, "We can never get enough of what we don't really need," and this is so true.

Look around you. Look at your clothes, your car, your home, your phone... they do not bring you happiness. They will all turn to dust just as your own body will. They will not be remembered. They are not truly valuable. The only true value we have is in our Lord.

He has offered us the great gift of eternal life in the Kingdom of God and all we have to do is to accept it. When our arms are filled with this Holy gift, we have no room for gifts of this world. I will pray that I see each one of you in Heaven with all the treasure we have stored up there — for there is no treasure here on Earth that compares. God bless!

ABOUT THE AUTHOR

Sterling Jaquith converted to Catholicism in 2010 before getting married. She and her husband live in Boise, Idaho with their four children Rose, Poppy, Violet, and Forest. She hosts the Coffee & Pearls podcast on Tuesdays and is the author of Catholic Mom Challenge and Be Merry.

She loves reading personal development books, drinking tea, taking bubble baths, and is constantly trying to learn how to be a proper homemaker!

Sterling loves speaking at conferences and retreats, sharing her conversion story and the message that we should all be striving for sainthood!

You can read more of her writings at www.Catholic365.com and www.catholicmom.com.

ACKNOWLEDGEMENTS

Thank you Jesus for letting me crash and burn financially for me to truly see what a slave I was to material things. When you lose the ability to pad your self-worth with stuff, you quickly discover that stuff never added to your self-worth anyway.

Thank you Mother Mary for letting me cry on your shoulder as I experienced the pain of consumerism detox. It is genuinely painful to detach yourself from the world but I am grateful for your patience.

Thank you to my entire family for putting up with me tossing half our stuff and continually asking, "Do you really need this?"

Thank you to my friends who have let me drone on and on about minimalism and who have answered my questions about large family and homeschooling logistics!

And lastly, thank you to all the Catholic Mom Challenge and Coffee & Pearls supporters. Your stories continue to inspire me. Your hard work makes me want to work harder. I feel blessed to be part of such a great community of Catholics.

Catholic Mom Challenge

Check out Sterling's other book Catholic Mom Challenge available at Amazon in both Kindle and paperback formats!

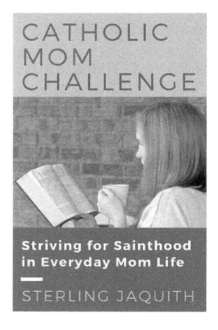

Filled with practical exercises and worksheets, this book is about helping moms figure out how to strive for sainthood among the piles of laundry, the mounting to-do list, and the stress of getting dinner ready!

The Catholic Mom Challenge system blends the power of Catholicism with discrete steps that busy moms can take to manage their lives while still striving for sainthood. This system works for everyone because it will teach you to always be refining what works for you.

Be Merry

A Catholic Guide to Avoid Anxiety and Depression During the Holidays

Check out Sterling's other book Be Merry available at Amazon in both Kindle and paperback formats!

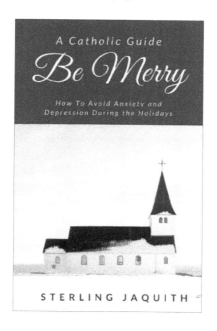

Do you feel anxious thinking about November and December? Are you worried about decorations, presents, and trying to survive your crazy family? This is not what Jesus intended for the season. Be Merry is a practical book about how we can avoid the common anxious and depressed feelings that wash over us during the holidays. Find out how to squish your envy bug, how to give your family to Mary, and more! It's possible to have a joyful holiday season! Come find out what can help you to set yourself up for success this year to draw closer to Christ and to find more peace in your life.

[i] Fr. Johns, Book Lift Up Your Heart: A 10-Day Personal Retreat with St. Francis de Sales (Ave Maria Press, 2017)

[ii] http://simpleandsoul.com/own-too-much/

[iii] https://en.wikipedia.org/wiki/Carmelites#/media/File:OCD_Zelle.jpg

[iv] https://www.rappler.com/move-ph/46933-new-year-resolutions-pope-francis-quotes

[v] https://www.psychologytoday.com/blog/hope-relationships/201409/the-psychology-behind-hoarding

[vi] https://www.adaa.org/understanding-anxiety/obsessive-compulsive-disorder-ocd/hoarding-basics

[vii] https://www.osv.com/OSVNewsweekly/ByIssue/Article/TabId/735/ArtMID/13636/ArticleID/10312/What-Catholics-need-to-know-about-making-their-homes-a-domestic-church.aspx

[viii] https://bootsandhooveshomestead.com/creating-a-domestic-church/

[ix] Marie Kondo, The Magical Art of Tidying Up (Crown Publishing, 2014)

[x] http://www.catholicnewsagency.com/column/the-importance-of-beauty-to-the-catholic-church-966/

[xi] http://www.theminimalists.com/20q/

[xii] https://www.becomingminimalist.com/a-parents-tip-sheet-for-owning-fewer-toys/

[xiii] http://www.theminimalistmom.com/2012/07/the3percent/

[xiv] https://www.becomingminimalist.com/a-parents-tip-sheet-for-owning-fewer-toys/

[xv] https://www.thespruce.com/avoid-having-too-many-toys-4114155

[xvi] http://minimalistathome.com/your-childs-messy-room-is-your-fault/?doing_wp_cron=1504628389.4581229686737060546875

[xvii] http://thestonesoup.com/blog/2010/04/how-to-setup-a-minimalist-kitchen-part-1-things-to-avoid/

[xviii] http://www.unclutter.com/spring-cleaning-your-garage-2/

[xix] http://www.theminimalists.com/workspace/

[xx] http://www.huffingtonpost.co.uk/rosie-leizrowice/the-psychology-of-sentime_b_15397710.html

[xxi] http://www.huffingtonpost.co.uk/rosie-leizrowice/the-psychology-of-sentime_b_15397710.html

[xxii] http://nourishingminimalism.com/2013/10/minimalist-seasonal-decor.html

[xxiii] Gregory Popcak, God Help Me! These People Are Driving Me Nuts! (The Crossroad Publishing Company, 2010)

[xxiv] Piers Steel, The Procrastination Equation: How to Stop Putting Things Off and Start Getting Things Done (Harper Perennial, 2012).

[xxv] http://www.livinglifefully.com/flo/flobethehappinessparadox.htm

CPSIA information can be obtained
at www.ICGtesting.com
Printed in the USA
LVHW111443170419
614518LV00001B/175/P